"What's going on? What's happening?" Bekah cried.

"We're being attacked! Pearl Harbor is being attacked!"

Bekah looked to the skies. Men on the *Nevada*'s deck swiveled their guns toward incoming planes. She saw Scott, standing behind one of the smaller guns. Blood was running into his eyes. "Scott!" She raced for him.

"Get down! Get away!" he shouted.

There was an enormous explosion. Debris flew up into the air, then cascaded back down toward the deck. It was a miracle that nothing hit her.

There was another explosion. The force knocked her backward; she tumbled end over end, shrieking, and when she finally ran into something on the deck, she thought every bone in her body had been shattered.

She wiped the dirt and blood from her eyes and saw that Scott had half fallen into the hole that had been blasted into the deck.

He was on fire.

Look for these historical romance titles
from Archway Paperbacks.

PEARL —1941— HARBOR

NANCY HOLDER

AN ARCHWAY PAPERBACK
Published by POCKET BOOKS
New York   London   Toronto   Sydney   Singapore

This book is a work of fiction. Names, characters, places and incidents
are products of the author's imagination or are used fictitiously. Any
resemblance to actual events or locales or persons, living or dead, is
entirely coincidental.

AN ARCHWAY PAPERBACK *Original*

An Archway Paperback published by
POCKET BOOKS, a division of Simon & Schuster, Inc.
1230 Avenue of the Americas, New York, NY 10020

ISBN: 0-671-03927-X

First Archway Paperback printing May 2001

10 9 8 7 6 5 4 3 2 1

AN ARCHWAY PAPERBACK and colophon are
registered trademarks of Simon & Schuster, Inc.

Cover art by Larry Lurin

Printed in the U.S.A.

IL 7+

In memory of my grandparents,
Kenneth P. Jones, Sr., M.D., and Lucile M. Jones, who
were on Maui when Pearl Harbor was
attacked. In memory of my aunt, Karen Beth Ingle, who
was on Oahu and saw it happen. In memory
of my father, who loved Hawaii all his life.

To Bekah and Scott Hardley,
Welcome to the great state of matrimony.

Acknowledgments

With thanks and *aloha* to my Pocket *ohana*: my editor, Lisa Clancy, and her assistant, Micol Ostow; to my *da kine* agent, Howard Morhaim, and his *da kine* assistant, Lindsay Sagnette. To my Hawaii *ohana*: Elise Jones, Hank Chase, David Wilkinson, Richard Wilkinson II, and Sandra and Bill Morehouse. *Mahalo* to the producers of "U.S.S. *Nevada* BB-36: A Legacy of Heroism," at KNPB Channel 5, Reno. To Jeff Mariotte and Maryelizabeth Hart: couldn't have, wouldn't have. To Jeff Thurman and Cap'n Hank Chase, thanks for the tech support. To Belle Claire Christine, my *menehune*, you are all the *aloha* in the world.

∾1∾

San Francisco
November 10, 1941

"Oh, my! What devastation!" Aunt Miriam cried, raising her hands toward the large clusters of diamonds at her ears. Her wedding ring caught the firelight and cast glimmering shadows against the banks of windows. "I've never seen such ruin and disaster."

The handsome young man seated beside Bekah chuckled. "It's pretty grim, isn't it?" He turned to Bekah with a warm smile on his chiseled face and said, "What do you think, Miss Martin?"

I think it was very unfair of my aunt to launch a surprise attack at zero hour, Bekah thought wryly as she smiled back at him. Raven-haired, square-jawed Peter Contner was easily the best-looking of all the many good-looking men Aunt Miriam had introduced to Bekah. He wore a swell-fitting dinner jacket that Bekah's friend Mari would insist was *da kine*, pidgin back home for "the best."

Peter himself was *da kine*—a Harvard man with a brand-new law degree, the heir to a lot of old San Francisco money, friendly but not pushy. Witty, too, in an understated way. And very polite. As Aunt Miriam would say, he was a catch.

Aloud, Bekah said, "I think my aunt has the best cook in San Francisco. And this carnage is the proof."

Bekah gestured to the vast array of nearly empty silver serving dishes shining against her aunt's heirloom lace tablecloth. In the candlelight, the poultry platter gleamed; the bowls of mashed potatoes, yams, and green beans contained only dollops of leftovers.

"I'll second that," Peter said. He wagged a finger at Aunt Miriam. "If you're not careful, Mrs. Jones, my mother will try to steal your cook."

"Hah. Let her try," Aunt Miriam shot back. "Nobody can spoil the help like I can. Now, if you'll excuse me, I'll see about the coffee."

Aunt Miriam rose gracefully from her chair. As she did so, Peter stood, too, and moved swiftly behind the pomaded, still-beautiful woman, who was dressed in a spangly dinner dress that clung in all the right places. Miriam Jones was still a "looker," as men said. And a widow.

"Thank you, Peter," she said, obviously pleased with him. She swept out of the dining room, a merry widow but not a silly one.

"Maggie!" she cried. "Has the chocolate soufflé fallen yet?"

"Oh, Missus!" a voice retorted. "You know my soufflés never fall!"

A bit shyly, Bekah picked up her spoon and polished it with her thumb, although, of course, all the delicate filigree in each sterling piece of the silver service was sparkling. Her aunt's palatial home always glistened, the wood banisters and floors waxed weekly, the chandeliers and windows washed at least that often. Fresh-cut flowers dotted the house in her spectacular collection of cloisonné vases.

"Alone at last," Peter said, grinning. Bekah felt the color rise in her cheeks. "Your aunt thinks she's pulled quite the caper, doesn't she?"

They looked at each other. Bekah saw the warmth and humor in his eyes and put down the spoon. She gave him a lopsided grin. "She doesn't want me to go back to Hawaii," Bekah explained.

He shrugged. "Well, based on our short acquaintance, neither do I. But that's not going to stop you, is it?"

"No," she said honestly. She liked Peter Contner, a lot. He had been a charming dinner guest.

"Still, I'm very flattered to be offered as an incentive to keep you here." She flared with embarrassment, and he inclined his head to acknowledge the truth of it. "She should have trotted me out sooner. I'd have you swooning in no time. But with less than a week until you sail . . ." He spread his hands, admitting defeat. "I'm not sure even I could manage it."

"How unfortunate that you had to dally back east," she teased gently. "I've been here for months."

"Yes. I was on my annual grand tour, visiting all my maiden aunts." He whistled. "I have a lot of relatives. What about you? Big clan back in the Territory?"

She shook her head. "Not really. I'm an only child."

"And so you've finished your nurse's training course, and your native soil beckons."

"My native soil beckons," she echoed. She gestured to the remains of their meal. "And contrary to what Aunt Miriam thinks, we *do* celebrate Thanksgiving. She didn't need to go to all this fuss."

"Have you got a fella back there?" he asked bluntly.

She sighed. "My aunt keeps neglecting to mention that I'm engaged to be married."

He lifted his brows. "She did somehow forget to tell me that." He eyed her hands, which were free of jewelry except for a small gold chain her father had given her for her high school graduation. "It

4

might make it a little easier on a man's ego if you wore a ring."

"I . . . I . . . It was lost." She paled. For a moment, the awful memories threatened to emerge. *No*, she told herself firmly. *I'm done with that.*

In the distance, a foghorn keened mournfully. Bekah rose from the table and moved to the glossy windows. Her view of the ocean was obscured by thick mist. She could see nothing of the lustrous city that had been her home for the last ten months. *In less than a week, I'll be home. And all this will seem like a dream.*

"San Francisco, home of the fog bank," he said, coming up beside her.

She shook her head. They stood in companionable silence. At five foot three, Bekah barely came to his shoulder. He smelled wonderful, and he was kind. She almost wished . . .

No, I don't. I'm going home.

Bekah thought of all the things she would be leaving—the hustle-bustle of the city streets, the restaurants and beautiful shops. The operas and plays. And movies. Back home, her family went down to Mr. Ling's grocery store once a month, to watch a movie everybody in the States had already seen. It had never bothered her, though.

"You don't want to go back," Peter observed.

She took a breath. "Of course I do."

"Of course you do," he said gently. When she turned to look at him, he said, "It's none of my business and never will be, regretfully."

"Here we are," Aunt Miriam said, gliding back into the room. She was followed by a tall, red-headed woman in a black-and-white maid's uniform who was carrying a coffee service on a tray.

Bekah and Peter went back to the table.

Soon after, she and her aunt wished Peter Contner a pleasant good night. Her aunt shut the front door, turned to her niece, and said, "Well, it seems you're in love after all."

Bekah blinked. "Excuse me?"

"If Peter Contner can't turn your head, no one can."

"Auntie, you should have told him I was engaged," Bekah said. "That wasn't fair to him."

"Oh, pooh." Aunt Miriam gave her hands a wave. "What's the saying? 'All's fair in love and war.' Besides, men like Peter can take care of themselves." She eyed her niece. "And he would take good care of you, Rebekah. You know he would." She sighed. "Harvard, rich as Croesus, travels all over the world."

"He's a catch," Bekah agreed. "But I'm still engaged."

"Well, I certainly hope that island boy knows how lucky he is."

"Of course he does," Bekah replied. She smiled. "And I'm lucky, too."

"Oh, my darling." Aunt Miriam looped a strand of Bekah's blond hair around her ear. "You're just like your father. So pig-headed."

At the mention of her father, a wave of home-sickness washed over Bekah. Suddenly, she wanted more than anything to be home, among the sun-drenched coconut palms and the heady fragrance of *pikake* blossoms and mangoes. Home, with Ian, and married. Mrs. Rebekah MacLaughlin.

"You look like your father, too," Aunt Miriam continued. "Where you two got that white-blond hair and those huge blue eyes, I'll never know." She patted her own chocolate-brown hair. Her hazel eyes were startling against her pale complexion.

"I guess . . ." She sighed. "I was hoping that you'd come to regard San Francisco as your home. I hate to think of you wasting away on those islands. Here, you have all the advantages—"

"I'm needed back home," Bekah said. "It's time to . . ." She searched for the right word. "It's time to go back to my own life."

Her aunt opened her mouth, then closed it firmly. She nodded. "Of course, dear. You know best." She kissed Bekah's forehead. "Forgive me for dangling Peter in front of you at the last moment. It wasn't in the best of taste."

"He was very flattered," Bekah informed her, chuckling softly.

"As he should have been. And if he had any sense

7

at all, he'd book a stateroom on the *Lurline* and woo you all the way to Hawaii." Her aunt tapped her chin. "And if he hasn't thought of it, I just might—"

"Aunt Miriam, you will do nothing of the sort," Bekah said, wagging her finger at her. "I'm . . . I'm marrying Ian as soon as I get home." She heard herself stammer and said more firmly, "I can't wait to marry Ian. I love Ian."

I do love him, she told herself.

You love him the way you always have—like a brother, a sharp little voice inside chided her silently. *Not in the way that he wants, or that you should.*

"We've known each other all our lives," Bekah continued, drowning out the little voice. "We're both island-born and raised. We couldn't be better suited."

And love will come. After all, I loved David with all my heart, and Ian is his twin.

"Oh, all right, dear. I know I'm being horribly selfish." At Bekah's questioning look, she added, "But I know Peter's mother is trying to steal Maggie away, and you know she's going to try a sneak attack while I'm with you in the islands. And I'll do anything to keep the best cook in San Francisco." She raised her voice. "Even if her soufflés fall flat as pancakes." She winked at Bekah.

"They never fall," Maggie called from the kitchen. "You keep that up, Missus, I *will* go work for Mrs. Contner!"

Together they reached the stairs.

"Well, Peter was my final salvo," Miriam said as they walked up the long, winding staircase. "I admit defeat. So get a good night's sleep. Tomorrow we'll buy you some decent clothes for your trousseau. No niece of mine is getting married in a grass skirt."

Bekah burst into laughter. "More clothes? You have no idea what island life is like, Auntie."

"Well, I'll have an entire month to find out, won't I?"

"You should stay longer," Bekah urged. "Once you're there, you'll never want to leave." She yawned. "It's warm, and safe, and wonderful."

At the top of the stairs, Aunt Miriam stopped. She cocked her head.

"Come here, darling," she said. She took Bekah's hand and led her into the master bedroom suite. The room was enormous, the soft cream and gold rug mirrored by the cream and gold satin sheets.

At the end of the elegant bed, a simple pine chest stood, its plainness a stark contrast to the richness surrounding it. Bekah had noticed it many times.

Aunt Miriam sat down on the carpet and lifted the lid, gesturing for Bekah to join her.

"This was Ma'am's hope chest," she said. "Your great-grandmother's. She was the one who married well and started the family fortune. Everything Ma'am touched turned to gold."

She smiled fondly. Then she reached in and

moved some faded pieces of thick material around. Bekah looked over her shoulder with interest.

"This was Ma'am's prized possession," she said as she revealed a plain wooden box. Carefully, she opened it, revealing a tiny oval of brownish pink. In the center was the head of a woman, her face in profile. Her hair was gathered up in curls. It was a ring.

"Oh, it's so beautiful," Bekah breathed. "May I?"

She reached out her hand. Aunt Miriam slid the ring onto Bekah's wedding-ring finger. "It's called a cameo," her aunt said. "I should have known it would fit you. Ma'am had very slender fingers. My finger's too big for it."

As if to demonstrate, she slid the ring back off Bekah's hand and placed it on the top of her own pinkie. It was a squeeze to get it down to the first knuckle.

Miriam put it back in the box. She looked at Bekah, who stared at the exquisite cameo.

"I'll bet you this ring that when we get to Hawaii, you'll see that everything has changed. That *you* have changed."

She patted Bekah's hand.

"You're like me, Rebekah," she concluded. "You won't be happy stuck out in the middle of the ocean. You need excitement."

Bekah felt a little lurch at the pit of her stomach. "I've had enough excitement," she said, more sharply than she had meant to.

"Oh, my dear, how thoughtless I'm being," Aunt

10

Miriam said. She reached out a hand. "Please forgive me."

"It's all right, Auntie," Bekah said, taking a breath. "I'm just tired."

"Then go to bed." Aunt Miriam cupped Bekah's chin. "Tomorrow we'll go shopping all day long. You'll be the talk of the islands in all your fashionable new clothes."

I am already the talk of the islands, Bekah thought. *Or, at least, I was. Maybe by now, everyone has forgotten about what happened and moved on to something else.*

Forgotten that David MacLaughlin is dead because of me.

"Sweet dreams, dear," Aunt Miriam said. "Get a good night's sleep."

"Good night, Auntie," Bekah answered, mustering a smile.

She went down the hall and into the room that had been hers for almost a full year. The blue-striped wallpaper bordered with yellow lilies had been chosen just for her, because it had reminded her aunt of her pale blond hair and deep blue eyes. The lacy four-poster "because you are the family princess."

Family murderess, Bekah thought as she lay down fully clothed. She stared at the ceiling and knew she dared not fall asleep.

If I do, the nightmares will come. And I can't take them any longer. I need to find some peace.

I need to go home and make everything all right.

∽ 2 ∽

San Francisco
November 11, 1941

That night, Bekah tossed and turned, listening to the pouring rain spattering on her window. Her mind drifted like a sea bird, across the vast, flat cane fields of the MacLaughlin Sugar Company back home, and Kaanapali Beach, the dusty little town of Wailuku. The images rolled over her like waves: her father in his white coat and horn-rim glasses in his office at Kula Sanatorium; her mother chasing after her silly flock of geese at their weekend house, less than a quarter mile away from the MacLaughlins' big house.

All that was waiting for her. The warm, fragrant evenings sitting on the *lanai* and listening to the MacLaughlin manager, Octavio Mendoza, playing slack-key. The delicious coconut pies Ian's mother made herself, winning prizes every year at the Maui Country Fair. She had never shared the recipe with anyone. But she'd told Bekah, "Once you're a MacLaughlin bride, I'll show you exactly how I make them."

Bekah pictured her little black cocker spaniel, whom her father had teasingly named Mybabytoo. As a toddler, Bekah had wheeled her first dog, Mybaby, up and down the halls of the sanatorium in a doll carriage, announcing to the nurses and doctors, "My baby. Bekah baby. My baby." So naturally, Mybaby's son was Mybabytoo.

She closed her eyes and smelled the sweet, sweaty odor of Pele, "her" horse at the MacLaughlin plantation, a high-spirited chestnut mare named after the fire goddess. How many miles had she ridden on Pele, picking fresh guavas off the trees and listening to David, on Lono, chatter about the sugarcane? And tease Ian, who was so lost in daydreaming one afternoon that he'd failed to notice an overhanging *kukui* tree branch and had ridden right into it?

It's a good life, she told herself. *Even if . . . if David won't be there to share it.*

Without warning, a huge sob heaved from somewhere deep inside her chest. Tears spilled across her temples to her blue satin pillowcase. Until this year, she had lived her entire life on Maui, and she had loved her island fiercely. To her, it was paradise—the lush *koa* forests, the abundant fields of pineapples, onions, and vegetables, and, of course, the cane.

Her first memory upon landing in San Francisco was that the city, while immense and thrilling—everything a mainland city should be—was as cold as the top of Mt. Haleakala before dawn. Fog and icy rain made her shiver in her aunt's raccoon coat when other San Franciscans admired the fair day in their shirtsleeves.

"Poor Hawaiian girl. You'll get used to it," Aunt Miriam had clucked sympathetically. "Your blood will thicken." She touched her niece's cheek. "And I know you don't believe it, darling, but your heart will begin to heal."

Perhaps her blood had thickened. Bekah couldn't remember the last time she'd borrowed the big, bulky fur. And her heart had begun to heal—or so she'd thought, until tonight. For suddenly, with a handful of days until she returned home, she didn't think she could live on Maui without David.

But I have to, she told herself. *I said I would. They're all waiting for me. Missing me. We'll be married on December twentieth, just five days before Christmas. Everyone will be so happy to see the little Martin girl finally marry into the MacLaughlins, just like they've been saying I would all our lives . . .*

But everyone thought my husband would be David. Never Ian. Not in a thousand years Ian. Tutu Lili used to say he would never stop daydreaming long enough to fall in love with a girl, much less marry one.

14

"I've loved you since you were born," David used to say. It was true. Three years older than she, David used to cart her all over the island. Down in Wailuku, they'd say, "There's David with the baby." And shrieking and laughing at the Hana pools, "There's that MacLaughlin boy and his *menehune*."

"And you *are* my *menehune*," he used to tell her. The *menehune* were the little people of Hawaii, the elfin fairy folk. They could be mischievous tricksters or benevolent little gods and goddesses who could perform miracles, such as prepare elaborate wedding feasts overnight or build sacred *heiaus* and dams. Bekah was like a tiny pixie, usually sitting on David's shoulders or being pulled in his Radio Flyer wagon—much to brother Ian's boyish disgust, and later, to his complete indifference.

David was Bekah's world. He taught Bekah how to climb *koa* trees and win sack races, and also how to box. When she gave him a shiner, her mother made her quit. But David sneaked her out to the cane fields, where they sparred with no one the wiser.

They learned Morse code together, and soon they could tap out entire conversations on just about any flat surface around. On the night of her nineteenth birthday, he had said, "I've loved you since you were born, and I'll love you till I die." He tapped out I L-O-V-E Y-O-U.

Then he had slipped her beautiful pearl engagement ring on her finger. He hadn't ever actually proposed—not said the actual words—nor had he needed to. At her request, that ring now lay in his grave, among the ashes of his body . . . and of their dreams of life together.

Bekah's throat had become so tight she couldn't swallow. People said that the mythical phoenix bird, when burned, rose from its own ashes. Her heart could be a phoenix bird. Her marriage to Ian would be different from the one she had imagined with David, but that didn't mean it couldn't be a happy one.

It'll just take some getting used to. I'll be the best wife I can be to him. And there will be babies, and coconut pies, and so much else. I'll be the mistress of a great plantation someday, and Daddy and Mother will have a lovely retirement playing with their grandchildren.

"Oh, David, I'm so sorry," she whispered. "I'm sorry I took it all away from you. From us."

Bekah cried and cried as the rains came down. She cried until she was exhausted. As her room began to lighten, she finally began to doze.

She wondered nervously if the terrible nightmares would return. They had plagued her during the first unbearable months after David had died. That was when it was decided that she should get away from the islands for a while.

"You've never been anywhere else," her mother said, and there was a wistful tinge to her voice that gave Bekah pause. She wondered—not for the first time—if her mother felt exiled living in Hawaii, as

did many of Janet [...]
father's fellow physic[...]
them as "the Sad Ladies[...]
magazines and talked endles[...]
on in the States—movie star g[...]
and goings of rich society people—[...]
lives were empty and humdrum. They[...]
come up with all kinds of flimsy reasons fo[...]
ing to the mainland, which was very expensive.[...]

What Bekah found ironic was that mainlande[...]
fantasized about coming to Hawaii. Wealthy people
brought enough clothes and servants to stay for up
to three or more months, if not in one of the elegant hotels in Waikiki—the Moana or the Royal
Hawaiian—then in the huge beachfront mansion of
a friend or relatives.

"I wouldn't go," Ian had said. He was sitting on a
large wicker fan chair from the Philippines, idly
sucking on a piece of sugarcane. "What have they
got over there that we haven't, that's going to make
you feel better? You're with your family here. Your
friends. You've got enough going on without trying
to deal with strangers in a big mainland city."

"My aunt . . ." *is like a stranger to me*, Bekah had
thought. "It's a change of scene," she told him.

He gnawed on the piece of cane. For all his love
of sugar, Ian had perfect white teeth.

"Ian, surely you can understand why I might
need some time . . . away," she'd replied, feeling

17

&

Martin's friends, the wives of her

ns at Kula. Bekah thought of

" They devoured fashion

ly of what was going

ossip, the comings

as if their own

r seemed to

r travel-

s hun-
walk
caused
ment of

red from
if the skin
races, like
s ever. The
with high
e color of a
t was nearly
impossible to forgiveness.

Finally, he shrugged and closed his eyes. It wasn't until she got up to go home that he had murmured, "We think you might consider marrying me."

"We" being his parents and hers. Ian had never said he wanted to marry her.

Neither did David, Bekah reminded herself.

The rains poured down, and Bekah finally dozed off.

"Well, it looks as if you made a conquest," Aunt Miriam said from the foyer when Bekah rose from her bed just a few hours later.

She blinked as she belted her jade satin robe and pushed her hair out of her eyes. Her aunt was standing at the bottom of the stairs with an oblong gold foil box tied with a wide red velvet ribbon.

Bekah's cheeks warmed as she came down the rest of the stairs and took the box. Her aunt, in a lavender dressing gown, took a step back and folded her arms. Peeking from beneath a bow the size of Bekah's fist was a tiny white envelope with "Miss Rebekah Martin" written in ornate lettering.

"Who are they from?" Bekah asked hesitantly.

Aunt Miriam grinned at her. "There's an easy way to find out."

"But..." Bekah took a breath and slipped the envelope from beneath the bow. The box was heavy and began to slide; before she dropped it, Bekah sat on the bottom stair and laid it across her lap. Then she awkwardly slipped a stiff white card from the envelope:

> *Hurry home. We love and miss you.*
> *With aloha,*
> *Mother MacLaughlin*

"That Peter," Miriam said with mock exasperation. "I had a feeling he wouldn't take no for an answer."

"They . . . they aren't from Peter Contner," Bekah murmured. She was acutely disappointed, but she wasn't sure why. Not in a million years had she expected flowers from a man who'd had dinner with her exactly once in her life.

"Oh, from your fiancé, then," Miriam said with approval. "That's even better."

"Yes." Bekah swallowed and put the card on the stair. "Well, from his mother."

"His mother?" Miriam's pencil-thin brows arched as she raised them, then she smiled politely. "Well, how nice. It's a real plus when a girl gets along with her mother-in-law."

"I always have," Bekah said. "She's my horse's godmother. Well, Pele's not really my horse." She decided that that was a longer story than she wanted to tell; to stem any flow of questions from her doting aunt, she pulled off the bow and tried to unfasten the red ribbon. But it was tied too tightly.

"Maggie, would you be a darling and bring some shears?" Aunt Miriam called to the cook as she led the way into the dining room. Breakfast was waiting for them in silver chafing dishes on a large antique cherrywood sideboard; the smells of bacon and chocolate filled the air with delicious aromas. But the uneasiness that the night had brought had tied Bekah's stomach in knots, and she wasn't sure if she could swallow so much as a bite.

"Here, Missus," Maggie said, bustling from the kitchen. "Oh, Miss Bekah! Flowers from a beau."

"My fiancé," Bekah said, a little too brightly. She took the scissors and cut the ribbon. "Well, his mother, anyway."

"The family," Aunt Miriam corrected. "They're very clannish over there, you know, Maggie. And I gather that the women are in charge of everything."

"Sounds like paradise," Maggie teased. "When you have your bridal shower, don't cut any of the ribbons on your gifts," she added, folding her arms across the bodice of her black blouse. "It'll mean you'll have a long labor."

"Oh," Bekah said, embarrassed.

"For when you're having your baby," Maggie continued helpfully.

"Margaret," Aunt Miriam said sternly. "This is not a fit discussion for a young lady."

Maggie sniffed. Then, as Bekah began to lift the lid off the box, both cook and aunt leaned excitedly forward.

"It's got to be long-stemmed red roses," Maggie breathed. "Oh, how romantic. Remember all those lovely roses your husband used to send you, Mrs. Jones? Any occasion. Oh, he was such a lovely man. It's so nice, your young man sending you flowers, Miss Martin."

There was a layer of white tissue next, held in place by a gold embossed medallion. Bekah carefully unfastened the medallion, which had been glued in place, and folded back the layers of tissue.

She smiled in faint but pleased surprise. It was not a bouquet of long-stemmed roses. It was a beautiful Hawaiian *lei* of *lokelani*, the miniature roses of Maui. The scent of the islands filled Bekah's nostrils and helped her forget the sharp odor of smoke that had filled last night's memories.

"Well, how unexpected," Miriam said slowly. "How very tropical."

"Very exotic," Maggie added.

Bekah lifted up the *lei* and placed it over her head. She breathed and found herself remembering a day when David had pinned a hibiscus behind her ear and made her pose for some snapshots. David was an amateur photographer, and a good one.

To clear her mind, Bekah said, "When we sail, we'll this throw this *lei* into the bay. If it washes to shore, then I'll come back some day. That's the custom back home." She touched the *lokelani*. "When we dock, we'll get so many *leis* they'll come up to our chins."

"It sounds like such a wonderful place," Maggie said wistfully. Aunt Miriam was giving her a full paid vacation while she was in the islands for a month. The cook was going to work at a dude ranch in Arizona to make some extra money.

"It is. It's the best place on earth." Bekah took off the *lei* and put it back in the box.

"Will this fit in the ice box?" Aunt Miriam said, handing the box to Maggie. "We should try to keep it nice for as long as we can."

"Sure, Missus." Maggie took the *lei* out of the box and cradled it carefully against her chest. "It's too bad we can't put it out somewhere. It's so pretty."

"Well, I can't exactly wear it shopping in San

Francisco," Bekah said lightly. "People would stare, wouldn't they, Aunt Miriam?"

"I suppose." She touched her cheek. "It's a lovely custom, though. But I guess it's one best suited to island life." She clapped her hands. "Well, let's eat a nice, hearty breakfast, Beks. We're going to hit every shop on Union Square!"

"That sounds like fun," Bekah said, stifling her yawn. She really wished she could try to get some rest, now that the sun had chased the shadows from her room. But her aunt was already deep into plans for their day, and she had been brought up to be polite and respectful of others' wishes.

Aunt Miriam checked the small round watch pinned to her dressing gown. "Soon it'll be time for Maggie's soap. What's it called, *Madame Cadenza?*"

Maggie huffed and drew herself up. "You know I don't listen to the radio when I'm on duty, Missus! Besides, the *one* soap I listen to is *Young Dr. Malone*, and that's only because Miss Bekah's a nurse."

Aunt Miriam moved to the sideboard and took the lid off the first chafing dish. "Hmmm, scrambled eggs just the way I like them. Not too dry, but not runny. Thank you, Maggie. You really are the best cook in San Francisco."

"That's what Mrs. Contner tells me," Maggie said, goading her employer.

Aunt Miriam shrugged. "I understand that Mrs.

Contner gives all her help time off for their radio programs."

"I heard she gives each one of them their own radio," Maggie shot back. She looked down at the *lei*. "It's a shame to cram this in the Coldspot."

"Then don't," Bekah said impulsively. "Leave it out in the kitchen so you can smell it all day. We don't refrigerate them back home."

"Do you even have refrigerators?" Aunt Miriam asked. Then she chuckled. "I'm only teasing. Big breakfast, Bekah," she said with mock imperiousness. "People are starving in Europe."

"God bless 'em," Maggie said. "There was another shipload landed last week at Pier 25. Norwegians, Poles, sad-looking people. Children as thin as matchsticks."

Aunt Miriam nodded. "I understand why our government is neutral, but . . ."

"You know those Japanese are just itching for a fight," Maggie replied. "On the one hand, they're invading China, and on the other, they're blaming us for all their problems."

"Well, we did set up an oil embargo," Aunt Miriam observed. Then she moved her shoulders. "Enough of that. I refuse to talk politics before breakfast."

"Good appetite to you," Maggie said. She headed for the kitchen. "I'm going to the market. I'll be sure to give Mrs. Contner your best if I see her."

"Do that, Maggie."

Aunt Miriam winked at Bekah. "She's just trying to frighten me, you know." Then she frowned and cupped Bekah under the chin. "You look so pale, darling. Are you feeling poorly?"

"I had a little trouble sleeping," Bekah said. "But I'm fine, Aunt Miriam. Truly."

"We can shop another day."

Bekah knew her aunt had a very busy social schedule planned for the rest of the week. Shaking her head, she assured her, "I'll be fine once I have some breakfast and a nice cup of coffee. You'll love the coffee back home, Aunt Miriam. We grow the best coffee in the world."

"Yes." Aunt Miriam cheered. "I'm sure it will be wonderful, dear. Now, I was wondering about another tea gown. Do you have tea dances out there?"

Bekah let her aunt chatter as they ate breakfast. She pushed some eggs and bacon around her plate. She found herself thinking about Peter Contner—*oh, not because I'm attracted to him*, she thought, *but because he has no idea who I am, or what I did. He thinks I'm just some young girl without a thought on her mind except her wedding. I wish I were that girl. I wish I could stop thinking about what happened.*

"Dear? Dear? Gloves?" Aunt Miriam asked. "For dressing up?"

"Yes, Aunt. We wear them back home," Bekah

said, amused by her aunt's continuing assumption that the Territory of Hawaii was like some outpost beyond the reaches of civilization.

"One wouldn't know," Miriam said. "When you got here, you were brown as a nut. I was shocked your mother let you go around without a hat."

"She didn't exactly let me," Bekah admitted. "She finally just gave up."

"You sound as if you were a different girl," Aunt Miriam said. "You've grown up here, sweetheart. No more rebellious little tomboy. Now you're a young lady." She beamed approvingly.

"Thank you, Aunt Miriam," Bekah murmured. "I'm glad you approve."

"Who wouldn't?" Aunt Miriam said.

David, Bekah thought. But David was dead, and so, apparently, was his tomboy "best buddy."

Bekah's eyes welled with tears for them both.

The day was packed with shopping. Aunt Miriam bought enough clothes to dress all of Bekah's former classmates at Punahou, the private girls' school she had attended on Oahu. Though she had missed her family during her schoolgirl years, she had cherished the opportunity to obtain a first-rate education, one that could rival the best mainland schools.

Then she had started helping more frequently at Kula and discovered within herself a love of medicine. She hadn't thought to do anything much about it until David's death, until her mother suggested she attend a nurse assistant's training program while she was in San Francisco. She wasn't really a full-fledged nurse, but she was going to get married and become a planter's wife, so it didn't matter.

Still, she was sorry that she couldn't pursue more training. She wondered what all her old girlfriends were doing now. There had been a number of engagement parties the same time as her and David's. But after the fire, she lost track of everyone as she withdrew into seclusion. Her mother had tried to keep her up to date, but she just couldn't listen to any of it. Of lives that unfolded the way they were supposed to, happily ever after.

At the end of the shopping expedition, she and her aunt went for dinner at Cliff House, the famous restaurant perched above the jagged ocean rocks. Aunt Miriam told her that sometimes sea lions serenaded the diners, barking for the fish they smelled cooking in the kitchen.

Tonight there were no sea lions. There were many romantic couples, however, smiling into each other's eyes as they sipped glasses of wine and lingered over mouthwatering desserts.

That could be Ian and me, Bekah thought, looking at a young, fair couple in evening clothes as Aunt Miriam greeted the maître d' by name and asked for the best table in the house. The couple's hands were intertwined; candlelight glinted off the man's gold band. He kissed the woman's fingertips and then nibbled on them. The woman tilted her head just slightly, gazing at him with a very different kind of hunger—one not satisfied by chocolate pastries or sugared berries in rich, sweet cream.

The maître d' escorted her and her aunt to a table with a breathtaking view of the vast, blue-gray waters. Sea birds wheeled in the dying sunlight. The gauzy beams shaded the water with pastel colors. Breakers hit the lavender rocks below.

They sat for a moment in silence as the sky was washed with salmon and silver and peach.

There's so much to see and do, she thought. *I can't go yet.*

Maybe it was because she was leaving that suddenly San Francisco seemed so vibrant and exciting. *I've lived almost this entire year in a fog,* she thought, *and not the fog of this incredible city.*

"Beks? Are you all right?" Aunt Miriam asked gently.

Bekah stirred. All her emotions were mixing up inside her. One moment, she couldn't wait to get home; the next, she wasn't ready to leave San Francisco. One moment, she was aching with misery; the next she was moved to tears of happiness by the natural beauty around her.

She smiled crookedly at her aunt, and then at the

waiter who was standing beside her with a quizzical look on his face.

"Miss?" he inquired politely. "Would you care to order?"

"The abalone is the best," Aunt Miriam suggested.

"I'll have that." Bekah handed the man her menu. "Thank you."

Her gaze returned to the couple. Her right hand was cupping the side of his face, and he was molding it around his cheek. They were glamorous, mysterious. The woman's dark hair was swept up and held in place with French combs. Jet beads glittered on her evening gown as she picked up her champagne glass and placed it against her husband's lips.

"Bekah? Aren't you hungry, dear?" Aunt Miriam asked.

She looked down at her plate and realized she had barely touched her dinner. Her aunt's plate was gone, and a second waiter was cleaning the white linen cloth with a silver scraper and a miniature dustpan.

"Oh, no, thank you," Bekah said, picking up her fork. "I . . . it's just delicious."

"I'm sure she'll catch up with me," Aunt Miriam said, as she touched her napkin to the corners of her mouth. "Especially if she wants some of your scrumptious chocolate pie."

"Yes," Bekah said. "I wouldn't miss it."

The man bowed his head and left. Aunt Miriam folded her hands beneath her chin and looked carefully at her niece.

"I've worn you out today."

Bekah cut herself a piece of breaded abalone. "I'm not complaining. Your car's full of new outfits for me."

"And that negligee and peignoir set is just perfect for your honeymoon," Aunt Miriam said happily. "All that caribou! You'll be a vision. David won't know what to do with you."

"Ian," Bekah corrected softly. "I'm marrying Ian."

"Oh, dear, I'm so sorry. Of course." Aunt Miriam blanched and picked up her small glass of port. "Ian. Well, Ian will lose the power of speech when he sees you in your lovely things."

"He's not very talkative to begin with," Bekah said. "David . . ." She swallowed hard. "He was the chatterbox."

There was a brief silence. "Oh. Then I'm certain Ian's the thoughtful, pensive type," Aunt Miriam said decisively. "It is true what they say, dear. Still waters do run deep. The quiet men. They're the ones with the big thoughts. I'm sure your Ian has a great intellect. My dear husband certainly did. And he was quiet in the extreme."

It occurred to Bekah that her aunt was comparing the twins and trying to reassure Bekah that she was marrying the better of the two. With a pang, she thought of David's huge smile and the way he loved to imitate Mr. Ling when he called him up to make reservations for the movie. "Ah, so, young Mr. David MacLaughlin! Swell hearing from you! You want see the movie? How many? Okay, you, Miss Bekah, and brother. Got you, Jackson!"

Mr. Ling kept very up to date with all the mainland slang.

"You're really lost in thought today," Aunt Miriam said. "And I'm sure you were dozing off on the drive over here." She knit her brows. "Rebekah, are you certain you want to go back?"

Bekah stirred, alarmed, wondering if her confusion was that obvious. She brought her fork to her mouth and thoughtfully chewed the abalone. She nodded at her aunt, who sat back in her chair.

"If you have the slightest doubt . . . if we get there and you change your mind . . ."

Bekah swallowed the savory morsel and took a sip of water. "I understand," she said.

"Think of me as your safety valve," Miriam assured her. "You're welcome in my house for as long as you like."

"I'm a trained nurse," Bekah said, not even sure why she said it. "Well, a nurse's assistant."

Miriam folded her hands on the table and leaned forward. "I know, darling, and it's a terrific accomplishment. You don't know how proud I am of you. I'm a society woman . . ." She gave a wave of her hand. "I organize charity balls, and I write letters. But you can make a firsthand difference, and that's just marvelous. I'm all for the modern woman."

She held up a finger. "But there's no need to make life harder than it is, Bekah. Lord knows, San Franciscans get sick, just like people in Hawaii. Probably not *as* sick," she mused. "You have all those tropical fevers. And the conditions are so much more primitive . . ."

Again, Bekah was taken aback by the image her aunt had of Hawaii. It wasn't like that at all. Or had she herself forgotten what it was like?

"Thank you, truly," Bekah said. "But I know what I want to do."

"But . . ." Miriam sighed. "Very good, dear. Now, how about that chocolate pie?"

"Which we have in Hawaii," Bekah said, grinning at her aunt. "And which we keep in our refrigerators."

"Which you have in Hawaii," Aunt Miriam said. "As cold as cold can be."

Smiling at each other, they clinked their water glasses.

The pie was indeed very scrumptious.

The best ever.

When they returned home, Bekah discovered another gold foil box waiting for her on Aunt

Miriam's grand piano. This time, the box contained a dozen long-stemmed roses, and this time, they were from Peter Contner. His note was brief:

> *So enjoyed our dinner together. Might I ask for one more, before you set sail?*
>
> *Peter*

Bekah went to bed with a little smile on her face. Of course she wouldn't go—it wouldn't be proper—but it was nice to be asked.

It's not as if I'm joining a convent, she thought as she drifted off to sleep. *I'm just getting married. For the rest of my life, to a wonderful man.*

For the rest of my life . . .

For the rest of the week, Bekah felt as if she were making up for all the months she had spent in San Francisco and barely paid attention to anything outside her nurse's training. There were concerts, parties, and more shopping, as Aunt Miriam decided they should purchase even more gifts for all of Bekah's family and in-laws-to-be.

Coyly, she decided that they should celebrate Bekah's graduation one last time and that Peter and his mother were just the people required for such an occasion. They had dinner at the Top of the Mark, a lovely hotel that reminded Peter of France, and his mother of Spain. Everyone commented on the extraordinary numbers of servicemen bound for Hawaii.

"War's coming," Mrs. Contner said. She frowned and bit her lower lip. "I worry about you two girls, out on the open seas."

"They'll be fine, Mother," Peter said. Tonight he remained somewhat distant, perhaps respecting Bekah's status as an engaged woman. Bekah was surprised to realize that she was a little disappointed.

Then it was November 15, time to sail on the sleek, white ocean liner. The *Lurline* was one of the luxurious vessels of the Matson line, renowned for their style and comfort.

The docks were flooded with porters carrying the last of the luggage to the staterooms and cabins, the splendidly dressed passengers in furs and natty overcoats. Well-wishers swirled around them, oohing and aahing as they came aboard to bid their friends *bon voyage*.

There were clumps of servicemen everywhere, laughing and snapping pictures of one another. Bekah wondered how many of them were bound for Pearl Harbor. Word had it that there were so many military men there that they outnumbered the locals many times over.

Once more, Peter and his mother showed up. He wore a dark gray raincoat and a dashing fedora, and his mother's black wool coat was trimmed with fox.

Aunt Miriam had booked a deluxe suite, and it was breathtaking—much nicer than the cheapest first-class stateroom Bekah had lived in on the way over. It had two rooms: a large sitting room decorated in French Provincial and a bedroom featuring two large beds, some comfortable chairs, a writing table, and a handsome dressing table. Atop the dressing table towered two large built-in jewelry chests, one for each bed. Beautiful Oriental carpets in blues, greens, and peach matched the upholstery of the chairs and the bedspreads.

"How nice," Aunt Miriam said offhandedly. She admired the bouquets friends had sent her and quickly riffled through the stack of telegrams beside a huge silver bowl of fruit.

"Let's sit," Aunt Miriam suggested. "Where's our steward?"

She looked around. Immediately, a man in a white jacket appeared, bowing slightly. "Yes, Madame?"

"Tea," she said, "if you please."

"Of course, Madame."

"Maggie makes the most divine tea sandwiches," Aunt Miriam said.

"So I've heard. And scones," Mrs. Contner replied.

"They're absolutely the best I've ever had," Aunt Miriam agreed.

The steward left. Aunt Miriam, who had taken off her coat and hung it on the coatrack in the corner of the bedroom, primped her hair. She stretched her legs forward and rested her hands on the arms of her chair.

"This will do," she said to Mrs. Contner.

"I can't imagine your missing Christmas," Mrs. Contner said.

"I have it on the highest authority that I shan't miss it," Aunt Miriam said, sliding a glance toward Bekah. "And in fact, I shall be attending the wedding of the season four days before Christmas."

"It all sounds very romantic," Mrs. Contner observed.

The steward returned with the ornate silver tea things. Aunt Miriam poured, serving tea all around, sugaring and creaming for Mrs. Contner, then turning to Bekah.

"How will you take yours, dear?"

Bekah's nerves were boiling over. She said, "Nothing for me, thank you."

"Me, neither, Mrs. Jones," Peter volunteered. "Miss Martin, one last promenade?" he asked, holding up an umbrella.

"In this weather?" his mother exclaimed.

"I . . ." Bekah wasn't sure what to say.

"Oh, go ahead, Bekah," her aunt prodded. "Mrs. Contner and I are about to arm-wrestle for Maggie." She mock-glared at the auburn-haired woman. "If I find any of Maggie's secret recipes on your table, I'll consider it an act of war!"

"Surely, Mrs. Jones, you can't expect a treasure like Maggie to go unappreciated. Leaving her at Christmas. How on earth is she going to shine at a dude ranch at Christmastime? It's just so strange," said Mrs. Contner.

"Well, I'm certain that after my niece is settled, she'll be offering Maggie a new position in the exotic Hawaiian islands," Aunt Miriam shot back.

Mrs. Contner sighed theatrically. "I won't be able to compete with that, I'm afraid," she admitted. She picked up the silver teapot. "More tea, Mrs. Jones?"

"Why, yes, Mrs. Contner." Aunt Miriam held out her cup. "Maggie also makes the most delightful *petits fours*."

"Let's get out of here," Bekah murmured. "Those two are going to keep at it until we sail."

"All right. We'll see you in a while, Mother," Peter said. "I'm off to propose."

"Good luck, dear," Mrs. Contner said cheerily. "Don't take no for an answer. You'll get a bride, and I'll get a cook!"

3

Don't take no for an answer? A bride and a cook?

Bekah wasn't certain she'd heard Mrs. Contner properly. But the woman was smiling calmly at her son as if she were reminding him to wear his raincoat. Seated in one of the comfortable upholstered chairs facing Bekah's aunt, she added more sugar to her tea and stirred.

Aunt Miriam had her back to Bekah; before Bekah could say or do anything, Peter swept her out of the suite and into the interior passage, which was still packed with people laughing and talking in loud, happy voices. The smell of damp wool reminded Bekah of wet dogs. Every now and then, a New Year's noisemaker blatted above the noise.

"Mother and I were just teasing," Peter said, before she could say anything. "About getting

38

engaged. Of course. But not about stealing Maggie."

"Oh." Her cheeks grew warm; she felt foolish for the prickle of alarm their banter had caused. "Of course."

"Because you wouldn't entertain such a rash proposal," he continued.

"Naturally not."

He peered carefully at her, appraising her, nodding to himself. "You haven't done your season, have you?" he said. "You're new to the whole social thing."

"The whole . . ." She realized he was talking about being a debutante—dressing in lovely gowns and going to a whirl of parties and dinners, usually for the purpose of finding a rich husband. They did a version of that in Hawaii—the dresses, the parties—but in such a small circle, there wasn't much choosing and selecting to be done. Matches were practically arranged at birth.

"No. We don't go in for that much back home. There's not a lot to our 'whole social thing.' "

"You've not met a lot of fellows, then." When she frowned, he continued, "I mean, you're not . . . well, actually, I find your innocence . . ." He trailed off. "I sound patronizing, don't I? Please forgive me."

"I always knew that I would marry Dav . . . Mr. MacLaughlin some day. I didn't need to be a deb or any of that. Let's just walk," she said, almost desperately. "To tell you the truth, I'm scared silly of the ocean, and I'm not looking forward to this voyage at all. I thought I would do better with Aunt Miriam along this time, but it's just as bad."

"Going to Europe must have been a horror for you, then," he said, then shrugged. "Except that I'm guessing you've never been."

"I've never been," she admitted.

"Let's walk. I'll be quiet."

Here the deck was exposed to the elements, and a chilly drizzle was coming down. Peter moved away and opened the umbrella. Despite the chill air, the hard wood deck was crowded with people. Red carpets had been laid down, and they were being soaked. Still, without the carpets, Bekah figured the deck would be as slick as glass.

The sturdy guardrails were dotted with moisture, and on the seaward side of the barriers, lifeboats creaked beneath tarps, suspended in midair. Crowds of passengers were lined up at the rails, tossing streamers at the well-wishers below. Traveling to the islands was exotic and novel, and only wealthy people or those with compelling reasons to go to Hawaii could afford to sail on the lavish S.S. *Lurline*.

As Bekah strolled in companionable silence with Peter, she noticed a large clump of Navy men in white uniforms with white caps on the forward lower cabin-class deck. They were laughing and joshing and posing for pictures.

Peter commented to her, "Look at all those swabs. 'Join the Navy. See the world.'" He sounded a bit off. She wondered if he was ashamed that he hadn't enlisted. But they were not at war—not yet—and many San Francisco men had told Bekah that as soon as war was declared, they would join up. She was certain Peter would do his best by his country.

She nodded. "We have a lot of military in Hawaii. Pearl Harbor, you know. There are Army barracks all over Oahu."

"Lots of men," he said, looking at her. "I suppose I should be jealous. In theory, at least."

"You should be jealous of my fiancé instead," she reminded him with a gentle smile, "if you were honestly jealous, in practice." Her merriment faded. "My mother told me most of the men on Maui have volunteered for duty with the Army. We have our own company training at Schofield Barracks."

"Preparing for war," he said grimly.

She nodded silently. "My father says it's coming. But a lot of people don't agree." She took a breath. "What do you think?"

"I have no idea." He took her hands in his. She and he wore gloves, but she felt the warmth in his grip and felt a thrill skitter up her spine. He was a handsome man. He lived an interesting life. He probably dated princesses and wealthy heiresses. And yet he was standing here with her. It was very flattering.

"Miss Martin, I was teasing you about proposing, that's true." He gazed at her and smiled gently. "But I want you to know that if you should find your home situation . . . no longer to your liking, I know your aunt would be delighted to have you back. And I would be delighted to show you my city. There are few places as exciting as San Francisco any time of year."

He raised his chin slightly and smiled, seeing sights she could only imagine. His voice dropped. "During the holiday season, it's magical. The lights, the parties, the store windows, all exquisitely decorated . . . I always make it a point to be home for Christmas." He gazed at her. "You should be here for it. You would be radiant."

"That's very kind of you, Mr. Contner," Bekah said, blushing furiously. "But I won't be back." She smiled, also gently. "Or if I am, I'll be accompanied by my . . . my husband." Her voice caught, but she kept her smile firmly in place. She doubted Ian would ever want to travel to San Francisco. He was content where he was; he would see no reason to go anywhere else.

"It would be wonderful to see you again in any case," he said gallantly. He smiled at her and gave a little shrug of his shoulder. "My mother and I are both relentless. If we want something, we see no harm in pushing to obtain it." He wagged his finger at her. "Fair warning: Some day she will most assuredly steal Maggie the cook from your aunt."

Bekah plucked up her courage and said, "Hah. You know what they say: Pride goeth before a fallen soufflé."

Peter laughed heartily. "Oh, you're a breath of fresh air," he said warmly. "I'll miss the chance to get to know you better."

A few feet from them, a very short woman was hugging a tall young man in a raincoat similar to Peter's. Her face came up to the center of his chest, and the effect was quite comical.

The woman was nicely, if somewhat shabbily, dressed in a black overcoat and a hat with a jagged feather and a black silk rose on the brim. She squeezed the young man as if she would never let him go.

"Is writing often," she said, squeezing him with each word. Then she thrust him away from herself and stared at him full in the face with searching eyes. "Is telling old Kaliskis how he is." Tears ran down her weathered cheeks. She pulled a huge purple and black handkerchief from her coat pocket and wiped her eyes. "Being careful."

"Yes, ma'am," the young man said. His eyes were creased at the corners as if he were trying to keep from laughing.

How mean, Bekah thought, disliking him on sight. *Her heart is breaking, and he thinks it's funny.*

Suddenly, bell chimes trilled across the hubbub, followed by a sharp blare of the ship's klaxon. A ripple of excitement ran through the throngs.

"Ladies and gentlemen, all ashore that's going ashore," called a man dressed in a white uniform and hat. He was carrying a little glockenspiel. As he called out, he played the instrument. "All ashore now, please."

The elderly lady burst into fresh tears. The young man took her gloved hand, shook it, then turned it palm-down and kissed the back of her dark gray glove.

"Mrs. Kaliskis, you've been swell," he said, in a thick New York accent. "But I'm going to be all right. You tell Father Georgiou you saw me off and I was fine. And that I can't thank everyone enough."

"Ah, you make such a fine priest," she said. She made the sign of the cross over his head. "Go with God."

The lady dried her eyes. The young man—a priest?—linked arms with her and walked her slowly toward the gangway, where uniformed stewards were escorting hordes of well-wishers back to the dock.

As they passed Bekah and Peter, the woman glanced up at Bekah and said, "I no am Communist, *da?*" and clasped the priest's arm tightly.

"It's all right, Mrs. Kaliskis," the priest said. He grinned at Bekah . . . and then he did a double-take. His eyes widened, and his mouth parted. He looked as if he were about to say something, but he continued only to stare at her, just to stare.

Bekah caught her breath. She hadn't realized on first sight just how handsome he was, but in a very different way from Peter Contner. In fact, he wasn't as handsome as Peter. But there was something about the shape of his mouth, his straight, dark brows . . . or was it how deep-set his eyes were or the little gold flecks in them? The heavy lashes?

She took in his features and tried to figure out what was so arresting about him. If she looked at each part of his face, she couldn't point to the individual thing that made him so handsome.

There was definitely something, though. Looking at him, it was as if time had swirled around the two of them and then simply stopped.

Peter turned to Bekah and cleared his throat. She ticked her glance toward Peter, who gave her a questioning look. When she looked back, the priest and the elderly lady had moved on.

"What on earth was that about?" Peter said.

"Did she say he was a priest?" Bekah asked quickly.

"I believe so. Do you know him? You two acted as if you recognized each other."

The klaxon blew again, startling Bekah out of

her wits. Her heart was pounding too fast. Inside her gloves, her palms were moist. *I think I'm going to faint.* She only said, "We should go back and fetch your mother."

He nodded. "She's going to be very disappointed that you're not staying and marrying me." He waited a beat, and then he smiled at her. "She'd do anything to get Maggie to work for her."

"Yes," she said vaguely. She couldn't help glancing over her shoulder, to see where the priest had gone. He was nowhere to be seen. *Is he the passenger? Or is it the elderly lady—what did he call her—Mrs. Kaliskis?*

Peter eased Bekah around and shouldered their way through the throngs headed in the opposite direction, toward the gangway. The laughter and voices were growing louder and more excited. Moving into the enclosed passage, Bekah was squeezed by those around her. Shorter than the majority, she found her face pressed into wet coat arms and shoulders. She was jostled this way and that; after a few moments, she realized she was growing more lightheaded. The world was beginning to spin.

Anxiously, she reached out and grabbed hold of Peter's arm.

"I'm going to faint, I think."

A gloved hand wrapped around hers, and she was pulled quickly through the crowd. Faces met

hers head-on, grimacing and scowling; voices said,
"Watch it," and, "Well, I beg your pardon!" as her
way was cleared.

Then she was pulled into a cabin that wasn't her
aunt's—it wasn't half as elegant—and she took a
breath as she stumbled against a small dresser.

"Easy, easy," said the deep voice of the man
beside her. "Are you all right?"

She blinked at her rescuer. It wasn't Peter at all.
It was the young priest.

Before she could speak, he said, "Sit down. I'll
get you a glass of water."

"No, no. My aunt —"

"Are you a passenger?" he asked.

She nodded, trying to pull herself together. Her
aunt would be frantic, wondering where she was.

She lurched toward the doorway. "I'm fine," she
insisted.

"Sit down," he said sternly, "before you fall down."

The room tilted. She closed her eyes for a
moment; when she opened them again, he was
standing before her with a glass of water.

"Drink," he told her. He bent down to hand it to
her.

It's the way he smells, she thought. *That was what
caught my attention on deck. Because it's wonderful.
Some kind of men's cologne. No, something that's . . .
him. He smells . . . alive.*

Quickly, she swallowed the water and handed

back the empty glass. Their fingers brushed, and she drew her hand away and put it in her lap.

"My aunt will be worried," she insisted. "I have to let her know I'm all right."

"Are you?" he inquired politely. "I can go find her and tell her where you are."

In a man's cabin?

"I'm fine." She took off her hat and smoothed her damp hair. "Really. It's just . . . I didn't sleep well last night."

"Me, neither." He grinned as if at a private joke, and she was shocked. Was he implying something . . . that she shouldn't even be thinking about?

She rose, casually putting her hand on the back of the chair for support. *Why on earth is this happening to me?* she thought. *Is it my nerves?*

"My aunt. I—"

"As you wish." He offered her his arm, just like a regular man. "I'll take you to her."

"Thank you, Father," she murmured as she laced arms with him, embarrassed to call someone so young "Father." By the way he was scanning the crowd, she wasn't sure if he heard her.

"There you are!" Aunt Miriam cried, rushing up to them. Bekah disengaged herself from him almost as if she'd been caught doing something wrong. As if he understood, the young priest moved away. "I've been looking for you everywhere! Did you get lost, darling?"

48

"I'm all right. Thank you, Father." She glanced to her right, where the priest had stood.

But he was gone.

"Oh," Bekah said softly, regretful.

"Excuse me?" her aunt said.

Bekah looked around. He seemed to have vanished; but in the crowded corridor, it would be difficult to find anyone. "Where are the Contners?"

"They left." She tilted her head and smiled with amusement. "Did Peter actually propose?"

"No." Bekah touched her brow. "That is, he said it was a joke. I . . . Aunt Miriam, I'm not feeling too well. Do you mind if I lie down?"

"You'll miss the tugboats," Aunt Miriam protested. "Oh, but dear, if you're unwell. Are you having a case of travel nerves? Peter said as much. He said you were afraid of ocean travel."

"Something like that," Bekah admitted. "I'm not the world's best sailor."

"Oh, my poor darling. Well, we'll be on the ship for less than a week." She patted Bekah. "Let's get these heavy things off and put you in bed."

"You go on ahead," Bekah urged her. "I wouldn't want you to miss the tugboats."

"Oh, *pfft*. I've seen enough tugboats to last me a lifetime," Aunt Miriam told her. "But I only have one little seasick niece."

"I'm not seasick," Bekah insisted. *Yet*, she thought anxiously.

However, Aunt Miriam insisted upon taking Bekah to their suite. The spacious bedroom reminded Bekah of her aunt's room back home—*in Auntie's home, not mine*—only the furnishings were more up-to-date. The bedspreads matched the greens and peaches of the exquisite carpet that spanned the two beds, a counterpoint to the upholstered chairs facing the feet of the beds, set at angles with a table between them. The table stood at just the right height for writing letters or playing cards. A wonderfully large dressing table, with the two big jewelry boxes topped by lamps, featured a green and peach skirt and matching seat.

There were three more shuttered windows—not exactly portholes—and Aunt Miriam set Bekah on the bed near the windows. She said, "You should probably have some fresh air."

Bekah remembered her nurse's training and took deep, calming breaths.

"I know air-conditioning is the rage, but I can't help thinking we'd all be better off with real, unconditioned air," Aunt Miriam went on. "Do you have air-conditioning in Hawaii?"

"We don't really need it," Bekah said.

"You see? My point. No one needs it."

"But yes, we do have it."

She helped Bekah unbelt her coat and take off her tam-o'-shanter. Bekah shed her lovely blue-gray traveling dress, black heeled shoes, stockings, and chemise. Their steward had already unpacked their things, and Aunt Miriam fluffed a lovely new flannel nightgown around Bekah as she tucked her into her twin bed.

"I'll get you some tea, dear," Aunt Miriam announced, sailing into their sitting room. "Maybe I should have brought along a maid or two. So many of our fellow passengers have."

She bustled back with tea in a brightly colored cup with Polynesian women on it. "This looks very Gauguin," she said. She handed the cup to Bekah. "Drink it slowly. And relax." She smiled encouragingly. "We're safe as houses on this ship."

Safe as houses. That was a phrase David used to say. Safe.

And now he was dead. And the ocean was large, and deep, and unending.

"Good?" Aunt Miriam asked, meaning the tea.

"It's delicious. Please, go watch the tugs," Bekah urged her. "Please. I'm just a little overwhelmed, is all." She grinned. "Scoot, Auntie. Please."

Her aunt frowned uncertainly. "You're sure?"

"Yes," Bekah insisted.

Her aunt dithered for a moment, then said, "All right. Perhaps you need some privacy."

She crossed the room, glancing at Bekah over her shoulder. Bekah smiled and waved her fingers.

"Go," she ordered.

Once her aunt shut the door, Bekah murmured, "The truth is, Auntie, I have no idea what I need."

She thought of the handsome young priest. A flare of warmth spread through her, and she was shocked at herself.

Rebekah Martin! He's a man of the cloth! And you're engaged to be married. Your future is settled.

She sighed and drank the tea.

4

Maui, Territory of Hawaii
July 10, 1940

"What do you want?" David asked. "Do you want to forget him?"

Dressed in a black Spanish hat with ball fringes, a black bolero over a blousy white shirt, and black gaucho pants, the older of the MacLaughlin twins looked just like Rudolph Valentino. Astride his horse, Lono, he led the way down the steep, winding trail to the back entrance of the MacLaughlin plantation.

He looked questioningly at Bekah. She shrugged. Her black satin Spanish gown was hiked up to her thighs, and she had taken off her tight dance shoes. She was riding Pele bareback. Her black lace mantilla was waving breezily around her white-blond hair, which had been coiled into a bun. She was nibbling on a piping-hot sweet-bean *manapua* from Tutu Lili. A cold *manapua* was junk; if you didn't eat them *wikiwiki*, they became nothing but hunks of oily dough.

After she finished off the sweet, tasty morsel, she said, "If it's not all three of us, it won't be as funny."

They both glanced at Ian, who was bringing up the rear. He wasn't listening. His Spanish hat was looped around the pommel, and, as usual, his attention was elsewhere. In fact, he was facing away from them, watching something in the distance.

"Ian?" David called, trying to mask his impatience. But Bekah knew David's mood very well. He'd like to throttle his brother. "Ian, will you at least try to learn the steps, or do you just want to quit?"

They were dressed for apache dancing. Bekah's mother had told them about the strange, wild dance, where the man would throw his dance partner to the ground. Then she would crawl to him and cling to his leg while he looked haughtily away. Theirs was to be a satire, tango-style, with both twins flinging Bekah around and her getting more and more confused about which one was which.

Tutu Lili had decided to take some of her dance students over Oahu way to perform for the rich Americans and movie stars at the Royal Hawaiian Hotel. Bekah was one of Tutu's dance students, and it had been Tutu's idea to ask the MacLaughlin boys to join in. Without checking with his brother, David had said yes for both of them. But it was painfully obvious that Ian wasn't very enthusiastic about the production.

He could have just said no. We've gone to all this trouble, and Suzuki-san down Wailuku way made our fancy costumes. The performance is in two weeks, and he still doesn't know our routine.

"We could try doing it just the two of us," she suggested as she licked her fingers.

David made a face. "It wouldn't be as funny." He grinned at Bekah. "Except to our friends, who know *you're* the one who pushes *me* around."

"Oh, hah," she said.

"On the other hand, it'd be funny if we took turns flinging each other like rag dolls."

"That's true." She looked back to see what Ian thought. He still had his back turned to her. "Ian, can you at least pretend to care?" she pleaded.

"There's a fire," Ian said slowly.

David nodded, even though his brother wasn't looking at him. "Papa said he was going to burn the first and second fields tomorrow. Maybe he changed it to today."

Cane planters burned vast tracts of sugarcane when it came time for harvest. The intense blaze burned away the thick stalks and left the sweet sugar inside. It was tricky; the wind had to be blowing the correct way, or you could have an out-of-control blaze on your hands.

Just then, the wind did shift, and Bekah smelled

the smoke in the air. *They must be burning the fields after all.* There was no cause for alarm. The MacLaughlin cane workers—Portuguese, Chinese, and native Hawaiian, for the most part—would be keeping a close watch on the fire.

"It's awfully windy," David said. There was something in his voice that caught Bekah's attention.

"But not too windy," she said nervously.

David smiled and touched her cheek. "Of course not, *wahine menehune*. My father wouldn't have ordered the burn if it wasn't a good day for it. Right, Ian?"

Bekah and David turned to Ian. He was examining his fingernails. Bekah rolled her eyes, and David held his hands out to his side.

They continued down the path, moving through dense clusters of fragrant red ginger. From this vantage point, they had a bird's-eye view of the roof of the sprawling plantation house, which had been in the family since the 1800s. The first MacLaughlins had been missionaries, but their sons and daughters became planters. Now the MacLaughlins were the largest producers of cane sugar on Maui. They were some of the richest people in the islands, and they had the huge house to prove it. Its roof was gabled and curved slightly upward, as was the tradition. The house itself was wooden, painted a sparkling white nearly every year. There was a curved drive-

way to the entrance, and on special occasions—
luaus and Christmas parties and such—the drive
would be filled with the cars of their visitors. Also,
the bicycles and mules of poorer folk, such as their
workers.

The brothers were expected to run things
together, and David was looking forward eagerly to
the day his father handed over the business. But
Ian . . . well, Ian never seemed to look forward to
much of anything. Not that he was dour. He just
didn't care about things.

"Look," David said. On the horizon, they could
see billows of smoke rising as high as Iao Needle.
They both watched for a moment. "That's an awful
lot of smoke." He shook his head. "Something's
wrong, Bekah."

He turned to his brother. "Ian—"

"It's not right," Ian agreed. "Either they're burning more than those two fields, or it's out of control."

"Papa, what are you doing?" David said under
his breath. "Ian, take Bekah back to the house."

"Don't be *lolo*," Bekah snapped at him. "We'll all
three go."

She looked at Ian, who calmly gathered up his
reins and murmured, "Duke, come on. We can't
hurry down the path," he cautioned the others.
"We're getting to the slippery part."

"Ian's right," Bekah told David. "We still go
slow."

David waved a hand. "While our plantation burns up? No thanks."

He clicked to Lono, and the horse started moving into the section of the trail that was covered with ancient, ground-down chunks of lava. He put his heels to the stallion's flanks. The large horse picked up speed and immediately began to lose purchase in the crunchy lava soil.

"David, *mo bettah* I go slow," Bekah said, unconsciously slipping into pidgin, which they often spoke together.

He gritted his teeth, ignoring her as he urged the horse on. "Lono, make for go home," he said.

Lono whinnied with anxiety. Bekah reached out a hand to steady him, but at that moment, David shouted with dismay as the horse scrambled and slid down the trail about seven or eight feet. Chunks of lava and rock tumbled with him.

"Lono!" David shouted, as if it were the horse's fault.

"Please, David!" Bekah gingerly made her way to his side. She forced herself to remain calm. "Please," she murmured.

Ian's mount whickered as it sauntered to a stop a short way behind Bekah, as if to make the point that hurrying was not productive.

David didn't seem to notice. He prodded the horse on. Miraculously, Lono made it, slipping and sliding all the way. When the horse got to flat ground, he took off, cantering toward the house, then speeding at a high gallop along the side. Mrs. MacLaughlin's famous protea garden was there, and as he plowed through it, Bekah knew there would be hell to pay later.

Ian sighed. He looked at Bekah. Then he flicked his reins, and Duke nudged Pele.

"We should keep moving."

She nodded. Then she guided Pele down the slippery trail. The mare raised her head and whinnied. Plantation horses grew used to the smell of smoke, but Pele was nervous. She shook her withers as she minced downward, and whinnied again.

"What do you think it is?" Bekah called to Ian.

"Nothing."

She turned around to look at him.

"David going off half-cocked, as usual," he added with a faint smile.

She blinked. She had never heard Ian talk about his brother that way; in fact, she'd never heard Ian talk much at all.

"But we should make sure," she said.

"We should make sure."

They finally got down to the flat part and picked up a little speed. Wordlessly, they skirted the protea garden. As they reached the front part of the house, Bekah heard a distant shout.

"Ian," she said anxiously.

Duke came up beside Pele. Ian said, "Now we make *wikiwiki*.' "

The rest was a blur of galloping and flames and terrible heat as the cane fields went up, row after row, as fast as if they were doused with gasoline. Of workers, running and screaming, some on fire, others throwing water on the impossibly hot flames. Of steam and raging heat, everything all around burning in mass confusion as men shrieked and horses panicked.

A man in a black cowboy hat dashing for the road—Octavio—and jumping into a faded blue pickup "fo get boss." The vehicle roaring off, with burned men in the bed, headed for the MacLaughlin plantation house.

Shouting for the volunteer fire department, shouting for help. Her obedient horse ordered back to the stable, Bekah found herself part of a bucket brigade, her costume ripped on each side up to her waist. The flames advanced like an army, and the brigade kept backing up. Men dashed from the fields as the fire swept over the landscape. Some of them were badly burned.

"Where's David? Have you seen David?" she cried to every field hand she saw.

The soot-darkened men looked at her with puzzlement. Visibility was nearly nonexistent; the ash was raining down like flaky gray snow.

The fire kept coming, and coming. Ian worked

silently beside Bekah and finally said, "Go back to the house, Bekah. David will have your hide if he finds out you were out here."

"Ian, he's missing!" Her voice was shrill with fear.

"I'm sure he's fine," Ian said.

"How can you be sure?" she screamed at him. "How can you just stand there as if nothing's going on?"

His face set, he passed his bucket to the next person and reached behind himself to take the next one from a short, wiry worker. He practically threw it at Bekah.

"Look at yourself," he said. "You're barefoot and you're half-naked. One cinder will send you up like a torch."

"But . . ."

"*Mo bettah* you stay out of the way," he continued, gesturing meaningfully at the bucket she still held in her hands. "You're holding up the brigade."

She handed her bucket to the man in front of her and stepped out of line. Ian moved up, and the man behind him took a couple of steps forward. Bekah swiped back her blond hair and glanced down at her hands. They were cut and bleeding. The shreds of her satin dress were covered with blood, water, and a paste of dirt and ashes.

She whirled around, then burst into tears and headed for the road between the fields to get out of the heat. She felt stupid, useless, and weak; and she was ashamed to go back to the house.

She had to zigzag her way across the field to dodge the fire. Men raced at her, flushed out by the heat. Finally, she heard sirens, but they did nothing to relieve her tension.

When she got to the road, she saw a man in a straw coolie hat racing toward her, waving his hands.

"David, David!" he bellowed. "Come *wikiwiki!*"

She raced to catch up with him. He grabbed her hand and half pulled, half dragged her behind him. Her feet kept leaving the ground; she tried to keep her footing and clung to him with both hands.

The heat bore down on them. She knew she should feel it, but she had gone completely numb.

Past fields of fire, the two raced toward some unknown destination. The man tried to enlist others in his cause, waving and shouting at them, but no one paid him any heed.

It seemed they ran for hours. The man was heaving with exertion by the time they stopped, and Bekah fell to the superheated ground on all fours, trying to catch her breath. The air was too hot to breathe.

As the man panted, he pointed.

Bekah tried to scream, but her throat was parched.

David was standing on top of one of the wooden

storage boxes the men kept tools and *bento* lunches in while they were working. Not to be used during a cane burning, of course, but here was one. It was about three feet tall, and the flames were crawling up the sides. A ring of fire raged all around it. It was as if he were standing on a pile of kindling, waiting to be burned at the stake.

"David!" Bekah rasped. She coughed.

"Oh, God!" David shouted. "Bekah!".

The man who had brought her to David darted forward to grab the young man, but the fire flared up and he jumped back. Bekah said, "Go for help. Go now!"

The man hesitated. She bellowed at him, "Go!"

He turned and ran without another word. She stared at David, searching for a break in the ring of fire. It blasted upward, concealing him from her up to his waist. He screamed.

Bekah was sobbing. She raised her hands, pulled them into her chest. Then she covered her mouth as the tears rolled down her face.

Then a breeze blew, and the flames in front of David rode it like a surfboard on a wave. She could see his knees, charred and blistered. It was their chance.

He said, "I can't move. I broke my ankle."

Their gazes locked. He was crying.

"Help," he managed.

For the tiniest fraction of an instant, she hesitated. She looked down at the burning ground and her blistered, burned feet, and she was afraid of how much it would hurt. Then she pulled herself together and reached out her hand, running toward him.

The breeze blew the other way, and the flames rolled back over him.

They rolled over him.

He was a torch; he was on fire; he was . . .

Aboard the *Lurline*
November 15, 1941

On the *Lurline*, Bekah opened her eyes to the darkness. The suite was still and quiet, and all the lights were off. As the tears slid down her temples, she listened for telltale sounds that her aunt was asleep in the other bed.

She heard nothing. Hesitantly, she sniffled and whispered, "Aunt Miriam?"

When there was no answer, she sat up slowly and wiped her eyes with the backs of her hands. Then she swung her legs over the side of the bed and got up, testing to see if the ship was rocking. On the voyage to San Francisco, the purser had assured her that on a vessel this immense, such a sensation would be minimal, if it was noticeable at all. Maybe it was just her imagination, but now, as she made her way across the dark suite, the floor seemed to tilt with every other step.

It took a bit of groping in the darkness, but she located their private bathroom and found the light switch on the wall. She was a sight, eyes bleary and red from crying. She had no idea how long she had lain, half asleep, mourning the dead.

Maybe it's too early for me to go back, she thought, slightly panicked. Even if it was, what could she do about it now?

Turning on the faucet, she splashed some bracingly cold water on her face. The white, fluffy towel was comforting as she buried her face in it. It smelled like flowers.

Somewhat refreshed, she saw that the steward had thoughtfully placed her toilet articles in the drawers of the cabinet. She picked up her mother-of-pearl-backed brush and gave her blond curls a few strokes. Then she brushed her teeth and padded back to the bureau by the soft bathroom illumination, where her clean underthings lay neatly folded in the drawers. She slipped some on and opened the closet on her side of the room.

After a few moments of pondering, she picked out a long gray skirt and a soft pink cashmere sweater set. She dressed, wishing instead for a hot bath. But she was hungry and, truth be told, in need of company as the memories kept replaying in her head. She knew from her voyage over that there was always something put out, somewhere, to eat, even if it was a simple basket of fruit.

But she wasn't certain if she could keep anything in her stomach. The vivid memories had made her shaky and slightly sick to her stomach.

Nothing will change, she told herself. *No matter how many times I relive it, David will still be dead.*

Though her feet were still scarred and ugly, they had healed well—a testament to her father's medical knowledge. Now she stepped into new loafers and checked herself in the mirror. She added her string of pearls and the charm bracelet Mari, her best friend, had given her for her sixteenth birthday. Her mother had sent her a gold charm of a nurse's cap for graduation. Aunt Miriam had given her two charms: one of the Golden Gate Bridge and one of a gold nugget, in honor of the California Gold Rush.

A bit shyly, she poked her head out of the suite and walked into the passageway. It was still busy with people.

A familiar-looking man with amber-colored skin, wearing a high-collared white shirt, approached her politely and said, "May I turn down your bed?" When she blinked, he said, "I'm Emilio, your steward."

"Oh." She nodded. "I'm sorry. Yes, please." Then she flushed. "Actually, I just got up. My aunt's bed needs turning down, though."

"Very good, Miss Martin." He inclined his head politely and went inside the suite.

Bekah was beginning to perk up. She was eager to reacquaint herself with the *Lurline*. As she recalled, they had a late-night supper buffet on the upper deck every night, near the shuffleboard courts. Maybe she could keep down a bowl of soup. And a glass of tomato juice.

A band was playing something dreamy. The music wafted over the fog as she moved from the interior passageway to the open deck. A young, well-dressed couple was walking toward her, arm in arm. The woman was glowing with happiness, and the man smiled at his sweetheart with such love in his eyes that Bekah averted her gaze, not wishing to disturb a private moment.

As the couple came abreast of her, the woman smiled at her and said, "We're on our honeymoon."

"Much joy to you," Bekah replied sincerely. She felt a pang of envy; then she thought, *Bekah, you dolt! You'll be going on your honeymoon yourself before long.*

"I'm engaged, myself," she said proudly. "Only we're from Hawaii, so I imagine we'll have to go somewhere else."

"Oh? Where?" the woman asked.

"I don't know. I'm leaving it up to my fiancé."

"I can't imagine going anywhere except Hawaii," the woman said. "Sheer Paradise."

"It is that," Bekah said. "Well, have a nice evening."

"Oh, we will," the woman replied, giggling as she looked up at her new husband. They wrapped their arms around each other and slowly walked on.

We'll be just like them, she told herself. *Happy and in love. Except that Ian won't be quite so showy about how much he loves me. He's not like that.*

But he does love me.

He really does.

She walked on, pulling her sweater around herself. She ought to have brought her coat. It was so cold out.

"Going my way?" a voice said from the darkness.

A figure stepped out of the shadows. It was the young priest, dressed in his coat and hat.

"We meet again," he said. "Feeling better?"

"Um, yes," she told him, but it wasn't true. "Thanks." The word "Father" stuck in her throat. *I'm not Catholic, and he can't be much older than I am.*

He peered at her with his deep-set eyes. They seemed to bore into her, as if trying to learn the secrets of her soul.

"Still shaky? Maybe you're sick."

She fidgeted as if he could read her mind. "Maybe."

"Something wrong?"

"No. Yes," she said quickly. A single teardrop

slid from her eye, and as she tried to brush it away, he did it for her. His fingertip was surprisingly callused, like a laborer's, but his skin was warm. Her cheek tingled where he'd touched it.

"Something's very wrong," he said.

"I'm not Catholic," she blurted.

He paused. When she said nothing more, he scratched his chin. He had a very sharp chin, with a dimple in the middle.

"Well, there are classes you can take. They're called catechism, and—"

"I mean, I . . ." The tears fell more freely. She turned away. "I'm sorry. I—"

"Hey, hey."

He moved to her side and gathered her up in his strong arms. His body was muscular, and she felt safe harbor in his embrace. That released the tension she had bottled up for so long, and she wept against his shoulder, pressing her face into the wool of his coat.

"We'll find someplace private," he decided.

She kept crying as he negotiated the twists and turns of the grand ocean liner. Hawaiian music lingered in the halls, and passengers walked past, smiling at what they must have imagined were two young lovers out on a promenade. Bekah kept her face concealed and tried very hard to stem the flood of tears. But she couldn't.

"We can be alone here," he said finally. "Kind of."

He sat her down in a large leather chair and brought the footstool up for himself. She looked around at the rows of books and the oblong end table beside her, the interior of the table filled with books. They were in the ship's library. On the other side of the room, a few other people were reading quietly, but the young priest had taken her to an empty section.

"What's up?" he prodded.

She sighed, sniffling. He reached into his breast coat pocket and handed her a white handkerchief. She wiped her nose and clutched the handkerchief between her hands.

"I . . . I'm getting married," she began.

"Oh," he said quietly. She blinked and stared at him. He looked flustered and cleared his throat. "Sorry."

"I . . . I was engaged, and he died. And they all expect me to marry into the family, so . . ."

He wrinkled his heavy brows. His mouth was pursed. His smell came to her again as he shifted his weight, and she wondered what it was that smelled so good, and how she could notice it at a time like this.

"You're marrying a dead guy?" he said.

"His brother." She pressed her fingers against the bridge of her nose. "We've always been together. It was David-and-Bekah, like one name. We always knew we would get married."

"You and the brother." He let his hands dangle between his knees. "The dead brother."

She started to cry again. "I shouldn't be telling you these things. But you were so kind to me today . . ."

"Kind," he repeated. "Oh, sister, have I got news for you. A dish like you . . ."

A dish? She stared at him. "You are the oddest priest I've ever known." Grimacing, she added, "Not that I mean any disrespect. To be honest, you're the only priest I've ever known."

"Priest," he repeated carefully.

"But I've got to talk to someone," she said desperately. "You see, they're all expecting me to marry into the family. Even Ian—"

"Hold it." He sat back. For a moment, he studied her face, then he shook his head. "You're getting married to someone you don't love—"

"Oh, I love him—"

He held up his hand. "Someone you don't love, because his family expects it?"

"It's more complicated than that."

"Oh. Is it?" he asked her, leaning forward.

"See, we're island people," she explained. "We don't have that many choices, and they all love me, and I love them, and of course my parents would be relieved, since it was all so awful after David died . . ." She trailed off.

"You're getting married to someone you don't

love," he repeated. He raised his brows again and craned his neck forward. "That's not complicated at all."

"It isn't?" she asked in a small voice. Then she waved her hands at him as if to erase the question. "I do love him."

"Humph." He looked completely unconvinced. "Listen, sister—"

"Scotty?" slurred a voice from the entrance to the library.

Heads turned. A tall, burly, brown-haired man in a naval officer's formal white uniform hung on to the jamb as if for dear life. His cap fell off as he swayed, then stumbled. "Scotty!"

The priest rose and walked quickly to him. He grabbed the man's arm and spoke to him in a low, angry tone.

"I am *not* drunk!" the other man boomed.

The other library patrons looked up with interest. One woman, swathed in furs, sniffed and wrinkled her nose. When she caught Bekah's eye, she said in a loud voice, "Riffraff. They shouldn't allow military men into first class."

"Hey," the drunk man shouted. "We're going to war, lady. What's *your* excuse?"

"*Well.*" The woman snapped her book shut and stood. "I shall report you. You *and* your friend," she proclaimed, including the priest.

Bekah reached out a hand and said softly to the

woman, "He's a priest. The handsome one, not the drunk one."

The woman was taken aback. "Oh?"

Bekah nodded, swallowing hard. "I think he'll see to that other man."

The woman adjusted her furs around her shoulders. Then she tugged on the end of her right glove and said, "I came on this cruise to ease my nerves. I've had a very difficult autumn."

"I'm so sorry," Bekah replied.

There was a commotion at the entrance. The priest was steering the drunk man out of the library. The man was a few inches taller and far heavier, and his legs were like rubber as the two men shuffled along together.

To Bekah, the priest called, "Sorry about this."

"It's all right," she assured him. "Thank you, Father."

The woman huffed. "I should report them."

"Please don't," Bekah pleaded.

"Men who get drunk in public are despicable."

"Maybe he's nervous about traveling at sea," Bekah pointed out. "I know *I* am."

The woman hesitated. Then she relented. "Oh, very well. But if I see that man behaving that way again . . ."

"I'll march right down to the purser's with you," Bekah promised.

The two women looked at each other. Softening,

the other one said, "I hope you'll forgive me, but I couldn't help overhearing what you were discussing with that young father. If I understood you correctly, you are marrying a particular young man to please your two families?"

"Well . . . I do love him," Bekah murmured, embarrassed to have the conversation again, let alone with a total stranger. *And what is "Scotty" but a total stranger?* She smiled faintly. *I know his first name. He's Father Scott.*

"Of course, you have affection for him." The woman smiled at her. "And may I say, I think you're doing the right thing. All this marrying for love." She gave her hand a dismissive wave. "Marriage is one of the most important institutions in our society, my dear. It is not a fairy tale. There are no Prince Charmings."

"Oh," Bekah said, feeling fresh tears at her blunt words. She swallowed them down.

"We are not princesses, and there is no such thing as true love. If more young women were as sensible about it as you appear to be, we would all be a lot better off."

"Are—are you married?" Bekah managed.

"I'm a widow."

"Oh, I'm so sorry."

The woman raised her head. Her eyes gleamed. "There is no need for regrets, my dear. I was a wonderful wife to Mr. Palliard. He had no cause for dissatisfaction, and he thanked me for my devotion on his deathbed."

She held up her right hand and twisted a ring bearing an immense, square ruby bordered by what had to be diamonds.

"His last act on earth was to hand me this ring. It was to have been a gift for our thirtieth wedding anniversary, but he died six days before the actual date."

Bekah's eyes widened. "It's beautiful."

The woman smiled. Bekah thought her face was brittle and cold. "Thank you, my dear. Believe me when I assure you that as long as your betrothed is a man of good character, you shall find satisfaction in your union. In all other aspects, frankly, one man is the same as another. They are quite interchangeable."

Bekah was stunned. *That can't be true. Look at my parents. They're happy.*

Bekah had no idea what to say. "Thank you for your advice. I have to go now."

"It's been a pleasure." The woman held out her hand. "I'm Ida Palliard," she said.

Bekah took it. "I'm Rebekah Martin. My fiancé is named Ian MacLaughlin."

The woman's eyes widened. "Of MacLaughlin Sugar?" When Bekah nodded, the woman chuckled. "I salute you, my dear. An excellent catch. Don't think for a moment about breaking your engagement."

75

Bekah nodded and turned away. The woman sat back down and opened her book.

In a daze, Bekah wandered. *Is that really the way marriage is? Is she how I'll become? Mother . . . isn't happy,* she admitted to herself. *But that's not because of Daddy. She just feels cut off from things.*

But she's cut off from things because of Daddy's job. If she didn't have him, what would she do instead?

After a time, **she found** herself out on the open deck. The wind whipped around, piercing her thin sweater, and soon her teeth were chattering. She looked out on the midnight sea, her mind whirling.

What am I doing?

"Hey, we meet again," said a voice. It was Father Scott, joining her at the rail. "Jeepers, your lips are blue." Without a moment's hesitation, he took off his coat and scarf. She was shocked.

He was wearing a naval officer's uniform just like the one on the man he had shepherded out of the library.

"Better?"

"Thank you."

He jerked his finger over his shoulder. "You need to get out of this cold. I was about to go to the late-night supper," he said. "You game?"

She paused. She probably shouldn't. It wasn't proper. But his smile was pleasant—there were dimples on either side of his mouth, she now realized, in addition to the one in the center of his chin—and his eyes really did have golden flecks in them.

"I won't bite," he promised.

She laughed. "All right."

His smile broadened as he offered his arm. "Then let's go," he said, "while the going's good."

∾5∾

Bekah was aware that a few heads idly turned as she and the priest who was a priest no longer entered the softly lit Veranda Café, where the late-night buffet was spread out. She couldn't help the little tingle of pride at being seen with this man. She knew he was handsome, and military officers in uniform were generally admired. Back home, officers were welcome members of high society. However, clumps of unruly sailors were another matter, which helped explain Peter's negative reaction to seeing so many on board the *Lurline*.

A band played a soft, Hawaiian-style fox trot as couples danced. Wicker tables and chairs surrounded the dance floor on three sides, the chairs covered with subtle pastels that matched the green and peach of her suite. The walls were trellised. Colored lights shone down on ice sculptures of hula dancers and a Hawaiian man playing a *ukulele*. The paintings of Polynesian women on the walls and the palm-filled nooks were vivid reminders that everyone on board the *Lurline* was sailing to the South Pacific.

"Let's sit over there," the man named Scott said, indicating a small table at the far edge of the dance floor. They walked toward it, past a couple who were dancing cheek to cheek. The woman wore a low-cut, bright red evening gown, and when she saw Scott, she waved lazily and gave him a fairly obvious come-hither smile.

He smiled back, oblivious of Bekah's disapproving scowl or the surprising flash of jealousy that vanished as soon as she realized it was there, like the green glow on the ocean at sunset.

What he does is none of my affair.

After he led her to the small, intimate table, a steward appeared and pulled back her chair.

"Would you like a drink?" her companion asked her.

She said, "A Coke, thanks."

"Same for me," he told the steward. "And, please, with the red cherries."

The man inclined his head as if Scott were the king of England. "Yes, sir."

Bekah scanned for her aunt. She didn't see her anywhere, and she wondered where she might be. The *Lurline* was a large and luxurious ship, offering all kinds of activities for her passengers. Aunt Miriam had probably gone to the writing room. She corresponded with all sorts of people, all over the world.

After the steward left, Scott said, "Why did you think I was a priest?"

She looked down at her hands. "It's a long story. The lady who was hugging you kept talking about Father Georgiou and what a great priest you were, and—"

His laughter was deep and resonant. "I'm a Catholic, but that's as far as it goes. And not a very good one, if you ask my priest back home. Begging your pardon, Miss. My name's Scott DeAngelo, Ensign, United States Navy."

"I'm Rebekah Martin."

"Engaged civilian, Territory of Hawaii." He held out his hand, and she took it. They smiled at each other, and she felt riveted. Her whole body was quivering.

What was I thinking? He's twenty times more handsome than Peter Contner.

"It's nice to meet you," she said, then looked down at the table. "You know what I mean." She laughed shortly. "I said some things that were rather private, because I thought you were a priest . . ."

"Hey, don't be shook up about spilling your guts," he said frankly. "In fact . . ." He checked his watch. "Jimmy's probably finished spilling his, too." She must have looked a little green, for he rushed to apologize. "Sorry, sorry." He rolled his eyes. "I wasn't quite done with my charm school lessons when I got my orders to head for Hawaii."

Clearing his throat, he gestured to the menu that had been placed at her left elbow. "What grabs you?"

She opened the menu. "Maybe some soup," she announced. "Or a shrimp cocktail," she added, delighted to find it on the menu.

"Nothing from the sea for me," he informed her, shaking his head.

"That must make it difficult for you on Fridays," she ventured. At his blank expression, she moved her hands and said, "Because of the meat. Meatless Fridays."

"Oh." He grinned. "We used to cheat a lot back in the old neighborhood. You know how it is."

"Oh." She didn't know what to say.

"My grandmother was a real stickler for the rules, but my folks cut corners a lot. I guess that's why I've only got two brothers and one sister." He raised his brows as if he had surprised himself. "Pardon me, Miss Martin. That was a little crude. I'm used to being around a lot of men. You know how guys are."

"Uh . . ."

"Would you like to dance?"

She hesitated.

He smiled encouragingly. "I'm pretty snappy. I won't step on your toes."

"Oh, no, it's not that," she said. "It's just . . ."

"I know. You're engaged. And I'm just some hick from New York, got a lucky break, and I'm sitting across from the most beautiful girl on this ship. So I'm thinking, What's the harm? Because you know and I know, ain't nothing gonna come of it, except a nice dance."

She grinned at him. "You're very persuasive."

"Me and the Fuller Brush man." He pushed back his chair. "Yeah, we'll do it?"

As if on cue, the music stopped.

"Folks, we've had a special request," the band-leader announced as he stepped up to the microphone. "For Mr. and Mrs. Richard Lexington, here's a beautiful Hawaiian love song."

Applause scattered throughout the room. On the other side of the dance floor, the couple Bekah had chatted with earlier stood and smiled at the group.

The steward arrived with their drinks. Each was garnished with a colorful plastic monkey clinging to the rim of the glass, a maraschino cherry stuck through its tail.

"Cheers," he said, clinking glasses with her. He took a sip, clearly savoring it. Then he took her drink from her hand and set both down on the table.

"We're dancing."

He led her to the dance floor and took her in his arms. Bekah moved into them, trying to ignore both the qualms of her conscience and the electric jolt that shot through her as she felt his breath on her temple. Even though they were dancing a respectful distance apart, she was very aware of his body. The warmth of it, and the intriguing fragrance. She saw the light stubble on his face and those golden highlights in his eyes. He was leading her with assurance, so that she didn't even have to pay attention; she glided with him as if they were two halves of the same body.

The strains of the song were lush and romantic, and he sighed, making her physically jerk.

"Sorry," he murmured. "Did I do something?"

"No." She closed her eyes. She thought of the surf at Kaanapali and how, if you weren't careful, the undertow pulled you under and you drifted out to sea. Scott's arms were not a safe harbor. They were the depths, and she'd better be careful, or she would drown . . .

"And for your information, Miss Green Eyes, I never saw that woman before in my life," he said huskily.

"Wh—what?" She tipped her head back to look up at him.

"The one who waved and smiled at me." His face was rosy. His lips were slightly parted.

"I didn't notice."

He grinned, and then his smile slipped away. "Rebekah . . . this is . . . different for me," he began. "Do you believe in—"

A man in a naval uniform hurried up beside Scott and tapped him on the shoulder.

Scott sighed. " 'Scuse me," he said to Bekah.

He moved away, and he and the man talked in low voices. Scott said, "It's always something with Jimmy. All right, I'll go check on him."

But suddenly the air was split in two by the piercing shriek of an air-raid siren. The band stopped instantly. In the interval between one howl of the siren and the next, several women began screaming. Men in dinner jackets stampeded toward the single exit; one burly gentleman pushed a frail elderly lady out of his way, and she fell.

The bandleader stepped up to the microphone, but the wailing of the siren drowned out his voice.

"Stay calm," Scott said. He took Bekah's hand and began guiding her toward the exit, making way for her firmly but not aggressively. His features were hardened with grim purpose, but he was not panicky or fearful in the least. Together they reached the elderly lady, and both leaned to help her up. Someone rammed into Bekah, and she went sprawling, shielding the lady as she fell to the floor beside her.

"Ladies, you all right?" Scott asked. He helped the elderly lady up, then checked on Bekah.

"My ankle," she said. "I'm sorry."

"Women's shoes are crazy," Scott grumbled. Then he winked at her and said, "Don't sweat it, kiddo."

He scooped her up and flung her fireman-style over his shoulder. Her bottom was sticking straight up, and if she hadn't been so eager to live, she would have insisted he stop so she could get down.

"We're going straight to the lifeboats," he said.

"But they haven't told us to," the elderly lady protested, her eyes huge and terror-stricken.

"No, ma'am, they haven't. But I'm telling you, all right? Please, do as I say."

"All . . . all right, Admiral," she said querulously. "You are an admiral, aren't you? With all that braid?"

"I know what I'm doing, ma'am," he said firmly.

"Yes, I . . . I know," the lady said.

"Good."

As they joined the crush struggling to get out of the room, a man in a ship's uniform strode to the bandleader's microphone and held up his hands. He shouted into the microphone, but Bekah couldn't hear a word he said.

The siren abruptly cut off in mid-wail.

"Ladies and gentlemen, I'm the executive officer of the *Lurline*," he said. "We have just experienced a false alarm. Let me repeat: this was a false alarm. I deeply regret the upset we have caused you. There is nothing to worry about. There is no emergency."

The band struck up its cheery tune once more, but at that moment, Aunt Miriam rushed up to Bekah.

"Oh, Bekah, thank heaven!"

"I'll be hanged," Scott groused. "This ship's as bad as the Navy. We had three false alarms on maneuvers last week."

"Please put me down," Bekah said.

"Oh." He chuckled. "Sorry."

He slid her down his chest and set her gently on her feet. Bekah swayed. A steward was escorting the elderly lady they had aided to a settee.

Aunt Miriam's face was chalk white. Her hands were shaking. "Oh. This is horrifying." She touched her forehead, and her knees buckled.

"Whoa, whoa, whoa," Scott said. He slung his arm around Bekah's aunt and led her to the same settee where the elderly lady was seated. One of the ship's officers, a man with sandy brown hair and a pair of tortoiseshell glasses, was handing the lady a glass of something to drink.

"Ladies, are you in need of assistance?" he inquired politely.

"My aunt has had a shock," Bekah told him, and realized how silly that sounded. Everyone had had a shock.

The man turned his attention to Aunt Miriam.

"Madame, may I get you something? A glass of port, perhaps?"

"How about a shot of Scotch?" Aunt Miriam replied. Bekah took her ice-cold hands in her own and covered them, murmuring, "It's all right, Aunt. It was just a false alarm."

The man left them.

Aunt Miriam said raggedly, "It was unconscionable of them."

"They're just being careful, ma'am," Scott said. "Better a few false alarms than the ship goes down with all hands."

Aunt Miriam groaned and covered her eyes.

At that moment, the officer returned, carrying a silver tray as if he were a waiter. He handed Bekah's aunt a stubby bar tumbler and gave another to Scott. To Bekah, he extended a glass of burgundy wine.

"Please, Miss, I must insist," he said. "You've had quite a shock, and a glass of wine will do you a world of good."

Bekah took a sip. She smiled at the man and said, "It's delicious. Thank you." He stood watching her, so she took another tiny sip.

As soon as he left, Scott took the glass from her and said, "That's not a good solution." She saw that he had not touched his tumbler. Aunt Miriam drained her Scotch and gave him her glass as well. Then she leaned back against the sofa and wiped her brow.

Scott sat down beside her and let out a whistle. "Man, that was something, wasn't it?"

"It sure was." She closed her eyes and took a breath, then opened them again. She said, "Do I know you, young man?"

"Auntie, this is Ensign Scott . . ."

"DeAngelo," he finished for her.

"My aunt, Miriam Jones."

"How do you do," she said, then touched her forehead again.

Scott said, "Please, ma'am, let me help you to your cabin."

"Thank you so much," she said appreciatively.

Aunt Miriam let him help her up off the sofa. He laced her arm around hers and began to walk very slowly. Bekah was shocked at how old and tired her aunt looked; gone was her vibrant aunt, and in her place, a small, stricken woman shuffled along beside the tall, strapping man. She was grateful beyond words that he was helping her aunt.

"I've been reading in the papers about Japanese submarines," Aunt Miriam said. "They could torpedo us."

"They could. They probably won't," he said frankly. "The whole world would condemn them. Even that heartless monster Mussolini. Excuse my strong words, ma'am."

"Of course." She regarded him. "Are you going to be stationed in Hawaii?"

Bekah's heart skipped a beat. *It's none of my concern.* But she listened hard for his answer.

"I'm joining my ship there, ma'am. I'm stationed on the U.S.S. *Nevada.*"

"Oh, isn't that the flagship of the Pacific fleet?" she asked, intrigued.

Scott DeAngelo shook his head in disgust. "No, ma'am, it's not. You're thinking of the *Arizona.* The *Nevada* is a bucket of bolts that should have been decommissioned years ago. It's the oldest battleship in the fleet. If the Japanese manage to sink anything . . ." He trailed off.

"They won't go after the *Lurline,*" he finished. "I can practically guarantee that."

They moved to the stairs, and he carefully guided Aunt Miriam down them. He was as careful with her as he had been with the elderly lady who had fallen.

"Here we are," Aunt Miriam said when they reached the door of their accommodations. "What a nice young man you are. So gallant." She smiled wanly, as if she was feeling her age.

"I try to be an officer and a gentleman, ma'am." He glanced at Bekah. "Most of the time, I fail miserably."

"You must join us for dinner tomorrow night," Aunt Miriam said. "Mustn't he, Bekah?"

"Aunt," Bekah hissed warningly.

"I must tell you, however, that my niece is

engaged to be married," she added mischievously. As she chuckled, the years slid off her shoulders again.

"I know she is," he said evenly.

Bekah glanced down at her hands, saw that she was twisting them, and lowered her hands to her sides.

"And I was sorry to hear it," he added, looking hard at Bekah.

"Most men are," Aunt Miriam riposted. "But do come to dinner. We're traveling alone, and we could use some masculinity at our table."

"Tomorrow night, then." He tipped an invisible hat and clicked his heels as Aunt Miriam fished in her bag and produced the key to the suite. She opened the door and went inside.

"Well. Thank you," Bekah said to Scott.

"Rebekah." He gazed at her hungrily.

She caught her breath. "What you heard . . . was not for me to tell you. It's between Ian and me."

"I can't pretend you didn't confide your heart to me," he said. "I never turn my back on someone when they reach out for help."

His words cut her to the quick.

"I . . . I did. I turned my back." She brushed past him and fumbled with the doorknob, let herself in, and shut the door behind herself. Forcing back the tears, she leaned against the door.

"Beks?" her aunt asked. She was sitting on her bed, facing the door.

"It's okay, Auntie," Bekah said miserably.

She knew he was standing on the other side of the door. He tapped it once, as if to say good night, and then his footsteps sounded in the hall.

"It's okay," Bekah said again, and she ran to the bathroom to cry in peace.

∽ 6 ∾

After she was assured that her niece had been crying because the false alarm had frightened her, Aunt Miriam had left Bekah alone.

"I felt like crying, too," she said. "The war is coming, Bekah. Mark my words. We were fools to sail now."

The false alarm affected the passengers of the *Lurline* in many different ways. The next day, some dragged around, the fun gone out of the voyage. Others seemed even more determined to have a good time. The cocktail lounge clinked with the sound of ice cubes in glasses, and the thick odor of cigar smoke permeated the passageway that fed into it.

Impromptu parties sprang up in the deluxe cabins and suites, and as Bekah walked past them, she smelled peanuts, hot canapés, cigarette smoke, and perfume. Her aunt was invited to two different bridge games. Women bought orchids from the florist to wear in their hair. A few men purchased souvenir *ukuleles* and strummed them lazily as they sunned themselves on deck.

The fog of the Northern California coast gave way to the fat, round orange that glowed down on Los Angeles. Long Beach Harbor was their only port of call before Honolulu. The talk of the ship was the party of San Francisco passengers who had decided to debark there rather than face the prospect of being torpedoed at sea. The incoming Los Angeles travelers heard the story of the false alarm, but most of them simply laughed at the absurd notion that anyone would dare to attack an American passenger ship. They hadn't been aboard. They didn't know how frightened everyone had been.

Unexpected danger is new to them, Bekah thought. *They've never had anything really terrible happen.*

Bekah stood alone at the railing, facing the bow, in her belted trench coat and a colorfully printed gypsy scarf tied under her chin. Aunt Miriam called it a *babushka*. She was wearing sunglasses, and Auntie had opined that she looked like a Hollywood movie star.

It was midafternoon, and the sun was shining. The waves rolled mightily in the dark gray sea, dotting Bekah's face with moisture and salt. The sheer size of the ocean amazed her. Her home was protected by the thousands of miles of water between it and the rest of the world. The islands of Hawaii were remote in the extreme; she had never thought of them as such, really—her family kept in contact with the mainland via telegrams and letters, and she and the other young people knew all the latest dances and kept up with the new styles.

They were not part of the United States; they were considered a foreign country under the protection of America. Many older native Hawaiians still remembered when the United States seized power and dethroned Queen Liliuokalani. Now the Americans stood on the brink of war against another foreign country—Japan—and apparently both countries found her country, Hawaii, a convenient place to wage their battles.

Bekah gazed out to sea. She had been searching for dolphins. There was none. She sighed and tucked the hair that had escaped her scarf back under the silky fabric. The wind had whipped the strands into a tangle; she was sure that beneath the scarf, her hair looked like a rat's nest.

"Penny for your thoughts," Scott said, walking toward her.

Bekah caught her breath. He was wearing his ensign's uniform; the stark white formality gave him a bearing he hadn't possessed the night before. His jaw seemed more chiseled, his brows and lashes darker. There were hollows in his cheeks, making him seem more of a man, not a round-cheeked boy. He looked tired. In his high, starched collar and black-brimmed hat, he looked older and more stately.

An officer and a gentleman.

Bekah held her hand against the crown of her scarf. She couldn't tell which emotion was strongest in her at the sight of him—joy, embarrassment, or fear.

She answered steadily, "They're not really worth a penny."

He scratched his chin. "Hmm, that's a new one. Okay, then give me two thoughts for the price of one."

Bekah turned away from the ocean and leaned against the railing. She decided to be a little honest. "I was wondering what to say to you the next time I saw you." She cocked her head. "What about you?"

"I didn't get any farther than being glad I would see you again. And I couldn't sleep for thinking of it." His gaze bored into her. "I know, I'm a chump. I suppose guys fall hard for you all the time."

Her smile was crooked and a little bitter. "You don't know me at all."

"I learn quick. I grew up on the streets, Bekah. I'm not some soft, innocent college boy."

She was intrigued. "Yet you are a college boy."

He looked over her head, to a place only he could see. "Life is strange, you know? Jimmy— that's my buddy, the one who keeps getting in trouble. Well, his dad was one of the richest guys in town. But he and his wife, well, they had all kinds of problems." He whistled. "Boy, did they."

He looked at her. "And Jimmy didn't have any friends. I don't know why. He just had this hangdog air about him. Like he was a loser, and always going to be a loser." He shrugged. "I dunno. It didn't seem fair, because who knew what he could become? So I became his friend."

"You felt sorry for him," she echoed softly, moved.

He considered. "No. It's more than that. I believe in Jimmy. There's a good fella in there. But he's all mixed up with his folks fighting and feeling like they're sticking it out just because of him. Which they are, and it's pitiful. He's smart. Anyway, his old man pulled some strings, got me accepted to the same college that took Jimmy. It was humiliating."

She was surprised at that. "Then why'd you go?"

"My ma. She was so proud." He gave her an ironic smile. "The family's not exactly college material. This was quite a step up for the DeAngelos. She thought the Virgin Mary had answered one of her novenas. My ma is real big on the novenas. I'll bet you two bits she's praying for me right now." He smiled affectionately. "And, to be on the square, I did it for Jimmy. I was scared he'd wash out on his own. So was his old man."

He wagged his head. "It was my idea to join the Navy, which made the old man very proud. Jimmy didn't want to, but between us—me and Mr. Toombs—we figured it might toughen him up."

"You've done an awful lot for him." She smiled. "Changed your life for him."

"Hmph." He sounded embarrassed. "Someone reaches out, I don't pull back." He frowned at her. "That upset you when I said it before. I'm wondering why."

"I'd rather not say."

Bekah turned back to the rolling water. She looked directly down to see the jets of white foam churned by the speed and size of the great ship. They looked like soap bubbles, mountains of them.

And then she looked up again and saw a lone dolphin, streaking about twenty feet away, breaching the water and belly-flopping back into it. Then it executed an amazing flip and gracefully crested the next wave.

"Oh!" Bekah cried, clapping her hands together.

The dolphin shot through the water, cresting again. It breached again, arching as it defied gravity and hauled itself away from the water.

"I never get tired of watching them," he said. "Sometimes a whole school will show up, follow a ship for hours and hours."

"You've been at sea before?" she asked.

He rocked on his heels. "Got my sea legs. Crossed the equator, even. Most fellows figure Hawaii for a cushy tour. The men got so bored the brass instituted all kinds of tournaments. Baseball, basketball. They've even got company boxers. How about that?"

"Jimmy must be looking forward to it," she said archly.

Scott's face fell. "He's already celebrating. You know there's certain things going on in Honolulu I would never discuss with a lady."

Like the bordellos the military allows on Hotel Street. She tried very hard not to blush.

"Like all those bars, all that liquor," he said, and she was so very glad that she hadn't spoken up. "He shouldn't be anywhere near that stuff. So what do they do? Send us to Hawaii."

She remembered his reaction when the ship's officer had brought her the glass of wine after the false alarm.

"You're very protective of him."

"I want him to die of a bullet wound, not a rotten liver," he said fiercely.

"Not to mention cynical," Bekah added.

He took off his cap and ran his hand through

his hair. His fingers were long, and his nails were trim. David's and Ian's were usually stained from picking *kukui* nuts. "Like I said, I'm one of the guys expecting a war. I figure it for a short stay in Paradise and then a long voyage through Hell."

He regarded her. "Your people, they planning on staying in the islands?"

"Of course." She was alarmed. "Where else would we go? It's our home."

"Thought your fiancé stayed in San Fran." He gave her a funny look. "That tall, black-haired fellow. Wasn't he the man making time with you before we set sail?"

"Making . . . he was not," she objected. "He's just a friend."

He whistled. "Then, baby, put me in your phone book."

Her mouth dropped open. "What?"

He pushed his cap off his forehead, making him look rakish. "Well, I must say, you two were pretty friendly."

"Oh, so that lady who was crying over you, was she your girlfriend?"

He scratched his nose. "Mrs. Kaliskis? I'm not sure. We only spent one night together." As she sputtered, he laughed. "Father Georgiou arranged it with her priest. I didn't have a place to stay after I got to Frisco. By train," he filled in.

"She was afraid we thought she was a Communist."

"She's from Russia. She gets that a lot." He shook his head. "Her son enlisted and went to fight with the Brits."

"She must miss him."

"He's dead," Scott said bluntly. "Germans got him."

"Oh. I'm so sorry."

"So, see, a young man comes to stay in her house. He's in the military, he reminds her of her boy . . . tears." He cleared his throat. "I tried to keep it light, but I knew what she was going through when we said good-bye. Reliving the whole thing. Imagining how he died."

"Oh, so you knew how she felt." She swallowed, ashamed of herself for thinking ill of him at the time.

He nodded, not catching her hint of sarcasm. He was too busy staring into her eyes, and making her wonder what he saw when he looked at her.

He sees my sunglasses, she thought, feeling foolish.

"But that fella wasn't your fella." He didn't so much as blink; he simply kept staring at her.

"No," she whispered. "He wasn't."

"He wanted to be your fella."

She looked up at him. Chills ran up and down the length of her body. The tips of her scarf tickled her chin, and she wondered what his fingertips would feel like there, or if they trailed down the side of her face.

"How do you know he . . . wanted to be my fella?" She took a ragged breath and felt herself falling right into his gaze. *He's a world*, she thought. *An entire world I'll never know.*

"Because *I'm* a fella." He pursed his lips and drew slightly away. "Are you really engaged, or is that just something you tell men to make 'em leave you alone?"

The spell was broken. She said indignantly, "I really am engaged."

He blinked. "And so happy about it," he said sarcastically.

She didn't answer for a few seconds. Then she replied, "Of course I am."

He gazed at her again. Her breath caught in her throat. He took a step nearer. She told herself to move away, but something compelled her to stay where she was. Her heart pounded. Every nerve in her body tingled.

She lowered her chin and kept her eyes focused on the center of his chest. His smell wafted around her; she closed her eyes.

I don't want this, she told herself.

But she didn't move.

His breath was warm on the crown of her

head. The wind and the shushing sound of the waves receded into the background of her awareness. Her lids fluttered like a sleeper's when she knows she's dreaming and she needs very much to wake up.

He took another step toward her. Eyes still shut, she sensed his nearness. Their bodies were almost touching. Bekah began to tremble.

He stretched out his hand and took off her sunglasses in a slow, fluid motion.

She blinked in the sun. Then he caught her gaze and held it; she could almost feel him willing her not to turn her head, not to move in any way. It was as if his hand cupped her chin and held her still.

She tried to breathe. She tried to swallow. All she could do was stare into Scott's eyes. The gold flecks shone in the deep brown. He was looking at her hungrily. *He wants to kiss me*, she thought, and she was both excited and terrified at the same time.

I am engaged.

She jerked away, stumbling. He caught her hand and yanked her hard against his chest. His lips crushed hers.

For a heartbeat, she allowed herself to respond. Then she jerked away a second time and slapped him.

"How . . . how dare you," she blurted.

"Miss Martin . . . Bekah—"

"No," she said. She grabbed her sunglasses from him and put them on. "Don't ever speak to me again. You are no gentleman. And don't come to dinner."

"Hey," he said.

"Don't."

She turned on her heel and half walked, half ran to the stairs. As she clattered down them, the tears came harder. By the time she reached the cabin, she was silently weeping.

Aunt Miriam will ask me what's wrong, she thought as she rapped on the door. *And I don't know*.

"Hey," Scott said behind her.

She whirled around.

"Don't complicate things, all right?" she pleaded. "My life's all set."

"All set?" His laugh was short and harsh. "I'll bet you're not even twenty-one. You don't have the first idea what your life is going to be like."

"I do," she insisted. "I'm going home. I'm going to marry Ian. We'll run the plantation and have lots of babies."

"And you'll die of boredom before you're thirty. *If* the war doesn't destroy your little version of Purgatory."

"Purgatory?" she repeated, bewildered.

"Beks?" her aunt called through the door. "We need to dress for dinner, dear. You should wear your new black velvet. A blonde in black velvet is twenty-three-skidoo, as we used to say." She chuckled.

"Just a minute, Auntie."

She pushed Scott away from the door and stomped down the hallway. Then she whirled on him.

"What are you talking about?"

He smiled at her. "You're a real firecracker when you get angry." He folded his arms and leaned against the wall. "You know what I'm talking about. You're scared, Rebekah Martin. Shell-shocked, just like a soldier in a war. If a bomb comes at a fella, he wants to hide in a bunker."

She raised her chin and squared her shoulders. "That's a reasonable thing to do."

"Not if there aren't any bombs. Then he's just a poor, frightened Joe on the way to the loony bin."

"Are you saying I'm crazy?" she flung at him.

"I'm saying you're crazy if you marry somebody you don't love. There's nothing safe about *that*. Just ask Jimmy Toombs."

"Yes, there is," she blurted. "Because—"

She stopped, horrified by what she was thinking.

"Because if he dies, it won't hurt. Or it won't hurt as much," he said. His large hand cupped her chin. "So you want to go through life not hurting, but not very happy, either. Just existing. That's my definition of Purgatory. Or worse. You deserve so much better. I can give you better. I know I can."

"Please," she said in a low, shaking voice. "Please don't kiss me again. Don't make me . . ." *fall in love with you.*

"Be brave, Rebekah," he rasped, running his fingers through her hair, caressing her earlobe, her jawline, her throat. Her skin was burning with each touch. Her heart was thundering in her chest; she could hear the blood roaring in her ears.

"Be brave, for me."

She shook her head. "I know what I'm doing," she said steadily. "And I'm marrying Ian on December twentieth."

For a moment, he looked as if she had punched him in the stomach. Deliberately, he dropped his hands and stepped away. "Then dress for dinner. Wear the black velvet. Put a flower in your hair, and smile. I want to remember you looking radiantly happy, like a bride should, not covered with tears and misery."

Cocking his head, he added, "Most of the time we've been together, you've been crying. Do you realize that? Do you really think you can go back to your islander and pretend you don't have any regrets?"

"I have plenty of regrets," she said. "Everyone does." She thought of her mother and her Sad Ladies. "And we go on."

"Why? What's the point? Who benefits?"

"The people who matter to us."

He looked very sad. "I matter to you."

She looked anywhere but at him. "*That's* crazy talk. We just met. I don't even know you."

"You don't need to. You love me. You loved me the moment you saw me."

"Don't be . . . don't be . . ." She covered her face with her hands. "I don't love you."

"Then it doesn't matter if you marry me," he said simply.

"*What?*"

He took her arm and led her down the corridor, away from her suite and toward his cabin. She stiffened, trying to pull away, but he held her arm.

"What are you doing?"

"Just getting some privacy."

He opened the door.

A haze of alcohol hung in the room.

"Hey, Scotty," Jimmy said, sitting up. He had been lying across his bed, fully dressed. An empty Scotch bottle lay on the floor. "Hey, pretty gal. Where'd you find *this* one, Scott?"

"*This* one?" She whipped her head in Scott's direction.

"Girl in every port, right, Scott ol' man?" Jimmy slurred, dropping his head back. He chuckled and fell back against the mattress.

"I see," she said bitterly.

"No. It's not like that," Scott said, holding out his hand.

"You're quite right. It's not like that," she shot back.

She turned on her heel and left.

Three hours later, a collective murmur went around the oblong first-class dining room. Those seated at each of the round tables stared transfixed at the stunning blonde in the hourglass velvet gown and long black gloves.

Bekah kept her focus on the high arches enclosing paintings of tropical birds and sailing ships. Below them, the banquettes of exquisite island flowers fanned beneath romantic lighting.

It was the perfect setting for couples to celebrate being in love.

Bekah felt her heart turn to ice.

Her aunt said, "You're causing quite a stir, dear." It was obvious she hadn't the slightest idea what had come over her niece.

Bekah saw, and found, her friend Mrs. Palliard from the library. She gave the nonplussed woman a brief nod and swept toward her and her aunt's assigned table.

This was her first night at dinner. She saw that there were no men at their table, only two other women, both older than her aunt. One was frail and thin, her face as delicate as china. She wore a high-necked, lacy gown and no accessories. The other was beefy, like a farm wife. Her brown hair was pulled back in a plain bun. She wore earrings of enormous clusters of rubies, and a tiara sparkled in her hair.

That made four diners; each table held six. The other places were minus their settings.

"Where's the young ensign?" Aunt Miriam asked in dismay. "Surely he's not standing me up?"

Their steward approached. He handed Aunt Miriam a white note. She opened it. Bekah was itching to peek over her shoulder, but she sat regally as the steward turned his attention to her, pulling out her chair.

"Oh, dear," Aunt Miriam said. "His friend is sick."

"His friend is drunk," Bekah bit off under her breath. But she knew how wrong it would be to discuss such a thing in public, so she held her peace.

"I'd snagged a young man to be our dining companion," Aunt Miriam said to the other two ladies. "Very young and handsome."

The ladies tittered. The frail one said, "Oh, it would be so nice to have dinner with a man." She looked at the other woman. "How long's it been since we've had dinner with a man?"

"At least sixty years," the other one shot back, and they both laughed heartily.

She held out her hand to Bekah. "We're the

Dover sisters, out of Omaha. I'm Maud, and this is Ethel."

"How do you do?" Bekah said.

Maud leaned forward conspiratorially. "We thought there'd be more men. You know, with the war and all."

Ethel smacked her sister's wrist. "Don't be a hussy. Pardon her, Miss," she said to Bekah. "She is not actually a floozy."

"Don't listen to her," Maud said. "We weren't always old maids." She chuckled. "Well, Mrs. Jones, you did your best. There's no man on the menu tonight. And your young girl with her glad rags on. Too bad."

Aunt Miriam was looking at Bekah curiously. She said, "Do you remember our bet?"

Bekah shook her head.

"Ma'am's ring." She patted her evening bag. "I have it with me. As I recall, I predicted the islands would look very different to you upon your return."

"We're not there yet," Bekah replied. She opened her menu. "Oh, look. Man's not on the menu, but abalone is."

"Steak," Ethel said, pointing a finger at Bekah. "You need good, red meat. Why, you're skin and bones. You're as skinny as I am." She laughed and waved their steward over. "No matter what this young lady orders, Joe, bring her a steak."

The steward grinned at Bekah and bowed to Ethel. "Yes, Madame."

The man took everyone's orders—Bekah pointed to the abalone and said, "The steak, please." Then Ethel appraised Bekah.

"You got a fella?" she demanded.

"I'm on my way home, to be married."

"Hot dog!" She picked up her fork and rapped the table with it. "Life without a man is a bunch of phonus balonus." She waved her fork back and forth. "I'd sooner cook for any man in this room than live another day with Ethel."

Ethel said, "Me, too, Maud."

Both sisters laughed merrily.

Maud leaned forward. "Is your fella handsome?"

Bekah nodded without hesitating.

"Dashing?" she persisted.

"Of course he is," Ethel said. "There he is!"

Bekah turned.

Dressed in a tuxedo, not a naval uniform, Scott stood at the entrance to the dining room. He saw her and made for their table.

"Hot dog," Maud murmured. "Hubba hubba."

"Oh, be quiet," Ethel said. "You'll embarrass the poor boy."

"Ensign," Aunt Miriam greeted him warmly. "I'm delighted to see you. I thought your friend had taken ill."

"He's doing better," he told her. Then his gaze

swept from Bekah's face to her bodice—or lack of one—and back to her face.

"What a man," Maud chortled. "Everything you described, and then some. Miss Martin, it's so nice to meet your fiancé."

Bekah touched her forehead as she realized the misunderstanding. "Oh, he's—"

"He's delightful," Aunt Miriam said quickly, making a moue of apology at both Bekah and Scott. But her eyes were gleaming with mischief. "Everything I could want for my niece."

Bekah burned scarlet.

"Thank you, *Auntie*," Scott said. "You're the bee's knees, yourself."

"We must have champagne!" Ethel cried. "Joe!"

"Actually, his name is *Royal*," Aunt Miriam whispered to Bekah.

"Actually, my fiancé's name is *Ian*," Bekah whispered back at her.

"Oh, let those two old birds have some fun." Aunt Miriam picked up her spoon and polished it with her thumb. A playful grin was ghosting at her mouth.

Their steward came over. "Yes, ladies?"

"Champagne!" Ethel said gaily. "The very best you've got, on our bill!"

"You can't believe how rich we are," Maud informed them.

"I don't drink," Bekah said in unison with Scott.

"*What?* Are you Methodists?" Maud demanded.

Ethel nudged her in the side. "Maud, if they don't drink, they don't. All the more for the rest of us."

"But I'll toast my lovely bride-to-be with water," Scott said, lifting his glass.

"Here, here!" the three older ladies chorused, clinking glasses.

Bekah closed her eyes.

I will strangle her for this, she thought.

But to Bekah's surprise, the ice around her heart began to melt. As the night wore on—and the three ladies became a little tipsy—she laughed at Maud's garbled slang and Ethel's stories about trying to frighten a bull out of their kitchen. It turned out they were cattle ranchers and, as Maud had asserted, extremely wealthy.

"You can come to our ranch for your honeymoon," Ethel told them.

"They're going to Hawaii, for criminy's sake," Maud said, sloshing champagne on the tablecloth. "Joe!"

The man was instantly at their service. "Yes, Madame?"

"You're a very hardworking young man, Joe," Maud said. "Are you married?"

He bowed from the waist. "Alas, no, Madame."

"Hmm." She raised her brows and winked at her sister. "Night's looking up, old girl."

Scott's startled, impetuous laughter rang out across the room. The other diners had begun to watch their table. At first, it had made Bekah nervous, but then she realized their expressions revealed envy, and maybe a little wistfulness.

Then someone sent over a fresh bottle of champagne, with a note that read: *To the beautiful young lovers.*

It was then that Bekah realized that she was, in essence, being disrespectful to Ian. It was wrong to masquerade like this. She said to her aunt, "I'm not feeling too well. I think I'll turn in."

"Oh." Aunt Miriam frowned. She touched her forehead. "Are you ill, dear?"

"No. Yes."

Scott rose and pulled out her chair. "I'll walk you back, darling."

"Oh. Maybe I'll just wait for you, Auntie," she backtracked.

"In our day, Papa would never let us be alone with a boy. We had to have a chaperone," Maud announced.

"And a gun," Ethel added. The two laughed uproariously.

"No, dear. You go ahead. Scott can walk you back." She picked up her champagne glass. "I'm having far too much fun with my two dear friends." She leaned forward. "My cook is at a dude ranch right now," she told them. "I had to get her out of

San Francisco while I was away, or one of my friends would have stolen her."

"When the cat's away, the mice will play," Maud chanted. "It happens all the time in Omaha. Once you find a good one, you've got to lasso 'em!" She raised her glass to Bekah. "Hurrah for Annie Oakley!"

"Now you're just being silly," Ethel chided her.

Scott took Bekah's hand and pulled her to her feet. She leaned down and kissed her aunt's cheek. With all innocence, Aunt Miriam kissed her back.

"Take good care of her, Scott."

Scott guided her out of the dining room. As they walked, applause scattered around the room.

Once outside, she pulled away. He exhaled.

"Oh, come on, Rebekah. Surely you don't believe that 'girl in every port' nonsense?"

"It doesn't matter," she said crisply. "I am engaged. And not to you."

"I hadn't forgotten that," he murmured. "But my proposal was sincere."

She kept her silence. He sighed again and said, "I'll walk you to your suite."

They walked in silence. After a time, she said, "How is Jimmy?"

"Remorseful. As usual." He sounded tired. "There's no liquor permitted aboard naval vessels. That will prove to be his blessing or his curse."

"Why do you say that?" she asked.

"It depends on how badly he wants to drink," Scott explained. "Either the temptation will be removed, or he'll figure out how to smuggle it aboard. And then, if he's caught, he'll go down in flames."

She shivered. "Please, don't use that expression."

"Sorry." He paused. "I'm in the same position, Bekah. I've got two days to win you."

"In two days," she replied hoarsely, "the temptation will be removed. Permanently."

"The island is small."

"I live on Maui."

"It's only a day's sail away. Shorter, if I can catch a ride on an amphibious plane."

"I'm getting married to Ian," she said flatly. Then she gazed up at him, keeping her voice as even as she could. "You wouldn't offer Jimmy a drink, would you?"

"Jimmy drinks because he's in pain, deep inside," Scott said. "Is that why you're marrying Ian? Because the drinks don't make him feel better."

"Don't start."

He took her by both arms and held her close. "Rebekah," he whispered. "Don't throw this chance away. It's out of the blue, I know, but sometimes the best things are the ones we least expect. The things we don't anticipate, don't plan for —"

I will not cry, she thought. *I am finished with that.*

Steadily, she stepped away and held out her hand. "Good night, Scott."

He must have sensed the finality of her words. His face fell. He took her hand and said, "I won't make this easy on you."

She turned away and walked down the corridor. Alone.

～ 7 ～

Near the island of Oahu, Territory of Hawaii
November 18, 1941

Bekah broke into a smile as the *Lurline* blasted its horn. Diamond Head stretched out its arm in greeting, and the pure white sand of Waikiki Beach sparkled in the brilliant tropical morning.

"Oh, my," Aunt Miriam breathed. "Bekah, Oahu is breathtaking."

Soon they would steam into view of Aloha Tower. Bekah eagerly anticipated the crowd that would greet the ship—and the loved ones who would be waiting to shower her with flowers and kisses.

I'm finally home, she thought, happiness flooding through her. She adjusted the sailor tie on her fashionable middy blouse, a stylish approximation of a sailor's uniform shirt, atop a dark blue pleated skirt. *This is where I belong.*

She was acutely aware that somewhere on the

Lurline, Scott was getting his very first view of Oahu. After their parting at dinner, he had kept his distance. Neither she nor her aunt had seen any sign of him in the ensuing two days. It was as if he had disappeared.

It doesn't matter, she told herself, firmly ignoring the tug at her heart. *It was a shipboard romance. Or, rather, it could have been one. What a disaster that would have been. This is the real world: Hawaii and my family. And my marriage into the MacLaughlin family.*

"It's like a dream," Aunt Miriam said wonderingly.

Pride and happiness surged through Bekah. With a bright smile, she threw her arms around her aunt and said, "I'm so glad you came, Aunt Miriam. You'll love Maui. It's even more beautiful than this island."

"Bekah, you are such a sweet angel," Aunt Miriam said fondly, kissing Bekah's cheek. "I can't wait to see your young man. And my brother. Imagine, soon he'll be a grandfather." She wiped her eyes.

Bekah laughed shyly as the klaxons blared again. "Not for a while, yet, Auntie."

"I must confess something," Aunt Miriam said slowly. "I thought . . . I was very, very worried about your returning here. You seemed to wilt at the thought of coming home. I really didn't think you should."

"I know," Bekah admitted. "I was worried, too."

"It wasn't fair of me to throw Scott at you. Please forgive me for that. I know it was hard on you."

"All forgotten," Bekah assured her.

Suddenly, she had the sure sense that someone was standing above and behind her, watching her. A warmth centered at the small of her back and spread outward. It was Scott. She knew without looking, even though she didn't know how she knew.

I won't look, she promised herself. *That's all forgotten, too.*

No, it's not, said the little voice in her head. *You can't stop thinking of him long enough to remember what Ian even looks like.*

Bekah raised her chin. She licked her lips and said to herself, *I have no regrets.*

The *Lurline* steamed on in the crystalline water. On the pristine sand, two crews of cocoa-hued men wearing *lava-lavas* of *tapa* cloth and anklets, bracelets, and crowns of pineapple leaves grabbed a pair of brightly painted outrigger canoes and dashed into the waves. At a shout, each team clambered in and took up paddles. Chanting in ancient Hawaiian, they paddled toward the much larger vessel. Cheers rose up from the passengers; some threw *leis*.

Finally, the *Lurline* reached Aloha Tower, an observation deck and clock tower, the tallest man-made structure on the island. A row of *hula* dancers swayed on the upper landing to languid slack-key guitar music. Someone behind Bekah yelled, "Hey, baby!" and she couldn't help herself. She turned to look.

It was Jimmy Toombs, and he was alone. He was hailing the *hula* dancers, waving at them with both hands. Bekah felt a pang and a flash of anger. She wanted to ask him if he realized how much Scott worried about him, and how often he let Scott down.

It's none of my business.

Streamers began spiraling from the railing, answered by streamers shooting upward from the docks, like little comets made of paper. Bekah leaned forward excitedly, searching for her family.

She spotted her father first. Tall, with blond hair like hers, Paul Martin cupped his hands around his mouth and called to her. She couldn't hear him, but she saw him and yelled, "Daddy!" as loudly as she could.

"Paul! Paul!" Aunt Miriam bellowed. She waved excitedly.

"Look, there's Mom," Bekah said loudly in her ear. Bekah's mother, dark-haired and short, like Bekah, wore a stylish shirtwaist of indigo *tapa* cloth. She wore a little straw hat trimmed with flowers.

"There are Ian's parents! And there's Mari, my best friend! We went to Punahou together."

"Oh, she's Japanese?" Aunt Miriam asked as Bekah waved furiously. Mariko had on a light blue shirtwaist, and her hair was pulled back in a ponytail. She wore socks and saddle shoes, and when she saw Bekah, she executed a cheerleader jump.

"Yes. Mari!" Bekah yelled.

Mari stood with Mr. and Mrs. MacLaughlin. Burdened with piles of *leis*, the adults waved and smiled while Mari shrieked and jumped with joy.

Where's Ian?

He was nowhere to be seen.

Surely he came.

She was baffled. She kept trying to locate him as she and Aunt Miriam began a very long wait to disembark. The delay seemed endless. The line for customs inched forward.

"There must be extra security," Bekah observed. "It wasn't like this when I left."

"It must be because of the war." Miriam looked grim. "It's all anyone was talking about at bridge."

Bekah thought of Scott. *If war comes, will he have to fight in some distant country? What if he . . . what if something happens to him?*

It's just as well I headed all that off at the pass.

She couldn't help but look every now and then for him. There was little else to do. In the distance, the Martins and the MacLaughlins were talking, and it began to look as if Ian hadn't accompanied them after all.

At last, Bekah and Aunt Miriam squeezed their way through the throngs at the base of the gangway. Mari screamed and ran at them, crashing into Bekah and crushing her cheeks with kisses. She threw a *lei* over Bekah's head and said, "Your bride dress came in last week! Oh, Bekah!"

"Mari, I missed you. I should've written more often," Bekah cried.

Then Bekah ran into her father's arms. He was wearing a blue and white *aloha* shirt and a pair of dark blue slacks. A lovely carnation *lei* dangled from his hand. He lifted her up and hugged her tight, then gently set her down.

"You grew up on me," he chided. "How could you do that?" Then he laughed and hugged her again. "*Aloha*, Bekah." He put the *lei* over her head and kissed her on the cheek. "My *menehune* child."

"*Aloha*, Daddy." She reached up on tiptoe and kissed him twice on the same cheek. "I didn't grow up at all, see? Same size."

"Mom," she said next as her beautiful mother embraced her and covered her face with kisses.

"My darling," her mother said. "I was so worried. There have been reports of submarines—"

"I'm okay," Bekah interrupted. She lowered her head to receive her mother's *lei* of *pikake* and orchids.

"*Aloha*, dear daughter," Mrs. MacLaughlin said

warmly, coming forward with her *leis*. "We're so glad you're home. Aren't we, George?"

George MacLaughlin smiled and kissed Bekah on the cheek. "Absolutely delighted."

And then, at long last . . . Ian.

He was standing half in shadow. He wore khaki trousers and a loose white shirt. His plantation hat sat straight across his head; David had worn his cocked. Otherwise, Bekah felt as if David were standing right in front of her.

She stood, waiting for his greeting. With a lazy smile, he hugged her, then kissed her, brushing her lips with his.

"Bekah, *aloha*," he said. "At last you're back. To stay."

He had not one but four or five *leis*, which he put over her head one by one. The scent of the flowers was delicious, and she laughed as she made a show of pushing them down, saying, "I can't breathe!"

Everyone laughed. Ian turned to meet Aunt Miriam. From Miriam's brief expression of shock, Bekah realized, too late, that she had never told her aunt about Ian's appearance.

The side that was untouched was handsome, in a gentle, English sort of way. His eyebrow and lashes were blond, his eye clear and blue. His nose was straight, just like his father's and David's, and he had the jutting MacLaughlin chin.

But the other side was a ruin. Bekah found herself remembering the first time she saw it, after the bandages were removed.

"It doesn't look bad at all," she had told him. And then, as soon as she could leave his hospital room, she had run down the hall into the ladies' room and cried for him.

As the family all hugged, Bekah with Ian, she hazarded a glance over her shoulder. She saw no sign of Scott. The *Lurline* eventually would travel to all the outer islands. Bekah's father had some business in Honolulu, and the MacLaughlins had their own yacht, so Bekah's parents had wired to say they would meet the travelers on Oahu. They were all going to stay at the Royal Hawaiian that night and return to Maui in the morning.

Mari joined Bekah and Ian, taking Bekah's other arm, and began swinging it happily. "You're back, you're back, you're back," she sang.

Bekah giggled. "Guess what? I'm back."

"She's back," Ian said with a faint smile.

They were walking toward the parking lot, while porters and passengers swirled around them. Carts of baggage nearly collided with one another. Horns honked.

"What was the mainland like?" Mari demanded. "Did you see everything? What about the Statue of Liberty?"

"That's in New York, silly. I was in San Francisco."

"Oh." Mari moved her shoulders. "But surely you traveled."

"A little. I saw the desert." She wrinkled her nose. "I didn't much care for it. Way too dry. Very desolate."

"Like Molokai?" Mari asked.

"Worse," Bekah said with authority. "But tell me what's been happening here."

"We're going to have a *luau* to celebrate your homecoming next week," Mari said. "*Kalua* pig and all the trimmings."

"Mari's been working on it for weeks," Ian told her.

Bekah beamed at Mari. "You're sweet."

Mari looked pleased. "It's too bad your house won't be finished in time."

Bekah blinked. "Our house? It's still not done?" Ian and his father had begun building them a small house just before she'd set sail for San Francisco.

"Didn't I write you about that?" Ian mused.

"You hardly wrote me at all," she said, making a show of pouting.

"I did," he said defensively.

"Anyway, no, the house isn't done," Mari informed Bekah. "But I'm sure things will move along faster. Ian won't want to live with his parents, now that he's going to have a roommate." She fluttered her lashes at Bekah.

"Mari!" Bekah squealed. "Shame on you!"

"Bekah . . ." Ian glanced at Mari, and something passed between them. Mari let go of Bekah's arm and said, "I'm going to go talk to your auntie."

Ian guided Bekah a little apart from the group. "We have to talk about some things," he said.

Her stomach fluttered. She felt guilty, and she knew she was right to feel so. She had been attracted to another man, and she had kissed him. She had loved him—

No, she told herself firmly. *I did not.*

She waited for him to speak, and when he didn't, she blurted, "Ian, what's wrong?"

"My parents aren't . . . they still haven't gotten over . . . it. Things on the plantation aren't going very well."

"Things . . ." she said carefully.

"My father's not managing the way he used to."

"Well, that's why he has you . . ." She trailed off, sensing she was navigating through tricky waters without a chart.

"You know more about running the plantation than I do," he said, sounding disinterested. "You know I never cared much about it. They're setting up Octavio's house for us for now," he said. "Do you mind?"

"Where's Octavio?" she asked

"Schofield Barracks. He joined the Maui Company. They're training for the war. Most of the hands enlisted. The ones who could savvy English, anyway."

She was taken aback. No one had told her about any of this in the letters that had come from home. "Then who's taking care of the fields?" He exhaled and pulled the brim of his hat down over his forehead as they walked into sunlight. She knew he was hiding his face as best he could.

"We haven't been planting as many fields," he said finally. "It seemed like the best solution."

He gazed at her. "It doesn't really matter. You know how rich we are. We could live off our investments for the rest of our lives."

"But your family worked hard to build MacLaughlin Sugar," she pointed out. "For generations, your family's whole life has been the company."

"You sound just like my parents. Me, I'm for relaxing and enjoying what we built. Don't you get it, Rebekah? We're rich. We don't have to do anything we don't want to do."

"But if we start spending and don't keep working the plantation, there won't be anything for the next generation," she murmured, a little shy about bringing up the idea of children. "And what about all the people MacLaughlin employs? Not just here but in the States, too. What would they do?"

"You worry too much," he said shortly.

Softly, she touched his cheek, then moved her

hand along his mouth toward the scarred side of his face.

His eyes narrowed. His face hardened.

"Don't," he said.

She froze. "What?"

"Don't touch me there, Bekah. Never."

He wheeled away from her and walked back to Mari. He spoke to her, and she patted his shoulder. Her expression, when she looked at Bekah, was one of sadness.

What's going on here? Bekah thought, confused. Her throat ached with disappointment. *This isn't how I pictured my homecoming at all.*

Mari and Ian walked over to her, and Mari placed Ian's hand in Bekah's. Then she kissed Bekah's cheek and wandered over to Ian's parents.

It's so awkward between us, she thought dejectedly. *It's not like it was before I left.*

She thought of Ma'am's ring, safe in her aunt's purse.

Maybe I'll end up wearing it after all.

By then, their porters had shown up with the luggage. They began loading it into the trunks of two large black Ford touring cars.

"Did you buy all the dresses in San Francisco?" Bekah's father asked affectionately.

A uniformed driver came around and ceremoniously opened the passenger door with a flourish. Mari said, "Let's ride together, you, me, and Ian."

"All right," Bekah said. Demurely, she held her dress at the knees and slid into the car, moving all the way across the broad burgundy leather backseat. Ian moved in beside her, followed by Mari. Bekah's father joined them, seated across from them in the pull-down seat.

As the car pulled away, Bekah glanced back through the rear window.

Her heart caught in her throat. Scott was standing at the curb, a sea bag at his feet. Beside him stood Jimmy Toombs, talking animatedly to Scott.

But Scott was staring at Bekah's car.

As if he knew she was looking at him, he pressed his fingertips to his lips and blew a kiss in her direction. It was not a flirtatious gesture; it was one filled with longing.

With *aloha*.

Bekah caught her breath. Then a taxi rolled up. Scott collected his sea bag and climbed in. Jimmy joined him, and the cabby slammed their door.

Bekah glanced nervously at Ian, who was idly looking out the right-side passenger window. He said, "I can't wait until all these people go back where they came from."

"The military boys?" Bekah's father asked. "I'm afraid that's not going to happen for a long time."

"Once they realize we're not getting involved in the European war, they'll go back to the States," Ian said. "And good riddance."

"They're protecting us," Paul Martin said. "When the war comes—"

Ian waved his hand dismissively. "It'll never happen."

"Let's talk about something else," Bekah suggested. "Are there any movie stars staying at the hotel?"

"I think Errol Flynn's there," Mari said.

Bekah lit up. The two girls shared an interest in Errol Flynn's movies. They both thought he was dreamy. They chattered about his films for a while. Ian kept looking out the window. He seemed to forget Bekah was even there.

After a time, she tried to bring him into the conversation by talking about sugar prices in San Francisco, but he kept his answers short, and the discussion fizzled.

"Here we are," the driver announced.

The Royal Hawaiian Hotel was also called the Pink Palace, and with good reason. The tall plaster structure was painted a vivid pink, and it towered above the palms arching around it like royal subjects on bended knee. As they reached the circular drive with the green-and-white-striped awning, Bekah thought about suggesting they come here for their honeymoon.

At the thought, she broke out in a sweat. *My wedding night, with Ian . . .*

Can I really go through with this?

The driver came around and helped Mari out first. Then Bekah. Then her father.

"*Mahalo*," she breathed, which was Hawaiian for "thank you."

As she straightened, she caught her breath.

A cab was pulling up behind their second car.

There are a thousand cabs on Oahu, she reminded herself. *What I'm thinking is impossible.*

He's gone.

She stood frozen to the spot. Her heart pounded. She was so anxious she couldn't breathe.

The cab door opened.

She swayed.

Scott stepped out. His head was down as he spoke to the driver. Jimmy got out next.

Then Scott raised his head.

He saw her.

She could almost hear him whisper her name.

"What's wrong?" Mari asked. She tracked Bekah's gaze and saw Scott. "Wow. Who's that?"

"He was on the ship," Bekah murmured. "Just another passenger."

"Hardly." Mari sighed. "What a dreamboat." She made eyes at Bekah. "Will you introduce us?"

"Of course."

Awkwardly, Bekah walked with Mari toward Scott and Jimmy. Scott's eyes never left Bekah's face. He didn't so much as blink. Bekah thought her legs actually might give way.

131

∽

"Mari Fujisaki, this is Ensign Scott DeAngelo," she said as calmly as she could. "And Ensign Toombs. This is my best friend, Mari."

Jimmy said, "My pleasure."

Scott bowed and said, "*Okage sama de.*"

"You speak Japanese!" Mari cried, delighted.

"Just a little." He held out his hand. "I hope we're not intruding. Jimmy has a friend who works here, and he wanted to say hello before we went to our billets."

"Where did you learn Japanese?" Mari demanded.

"I been around," Scott said modestly. He looked at Bekah. "Is your fiancé here?"

"Yes, I . . ." She looked around. Ian was just getting out of the car. "Here he comes now."

"Scott," Aunt Miriam said delightedly as she came abreast of the man. "We thought you'd fallen overboard."

"I wasn't feeling well," Jimmy told her. "I was . . . seasick."

How smooth, Bekah thought, disgusted.

"Oh, dear." She clicked her tongue in sympathy. "They have things for that."

"Yes, ma'am," Jimmy said.

The rest of the adults approached. Aunt Miriam said to Ian's father, "This is Scott DeAngelo. He was our chaperone on board. We had a most delightful dinner together."

Bekah ticked her gaze to Ian, who appeared completely uninterested in the conversation. In fact, he yawned and glanced at his watch.

"How about another one tonight?" Mr. MacLaughlin boomed. "I'm all for the military presence here on the islands. It'd be a pleasure to have dinner with you two men."

"Oh, George," Mrs. MacLaughlin said, "these young ensigns don't want to eat dinner with a bunch of stuffy old people."

"Hey," Mari protested, then looked flustered.

"Thanks very much, but I already have plans," Jimmy said.

Scott looked at Bekah. "I'd be delighted."

"We'll be in the lobby at eight," Mr. MacLaughlin announced. "Good for you, Ensign?"

Scott shook hands with him. "Yes, sir, I'll see you then."

He clicked his heels with military precision, bowed to the ladies, and walked into the hotel.

"Nice kid," Mr. MacLaughlin said. "Wouldn't have picked him for an officer with that low-class accent, though."

"He went to college," Bekah said quickly. Then she cleared her throat. "So he told me, at dinner."

"Well, I'd love to go in and get settled," Aunt Miriam said, deftly changing the subject. "It certainly would be nice if the land would stop rocking back and forth."

Bekah nodded. "I feel it, too."

"The swaying will wear off in a day or two," Dr. Martin said. "Your inner ear has accustomed itself to being off-balance."

What about the rest of me? Bekah thought. *Everything else is feeling off-balance, too.*

She glanced at Ian, who said idly, "I could use a nap."

Then they all trooped inside.

∽8∽

Oahu, Territory of Hawaii
November 18, 1941

Bekah and Mari shared a room at the Royal
Hawaiian, with Aunt Miriam booked into her own
separate quarters. Mari ogled Bekah's new clothes
with envy, holding up her black velvet evening gown.

They walked down the stairs together, and
Bekah thought about confiding in Mari. She had
been her best friend. She had held Bekah at David's
funeral, then cried with her all that night.

Mari was the only one who knew that the night
before she left for San Francisco, Bekah had driven
out to his grave and lain across it and tapped to his
spirit in Morse code: I L-O-V-E Y-O-U.

But now, all Mari could do was prattle on about
what a dreamboat Scott was. She had no sense of
Bekah's discomfort or unhappiness. Finally, when
Bekah couldn't stand it anymore, she blurted out,
"What's wrong with Ian?"

Mari looked startled. "What do you mean?"

"He doesn't seem very happy to see me."

Her friend laughed. "Bekah, have you forgotten what Ian's like? He's just being Ian."

"The plantation," she said. "How is it?"

Mari sobered. "Not good. The MacLaughlins need you, Bekah. They need something to be happy about. I know his mother's looking forward to the wedding." She tugged on Bekah's arm as they reached the bottom of the stairs. "Wow."

Scott was standing all alone in the lobby, his cap under his arm. His profile was silhouetted against a large bouquet of white chrysanthemums.

Then Ian sauntered up, in a white dinner jacket. He saw Bekah and Mari and waved lazily. Scott, however, walked up to greet them both.

"Ladies," he said, inclining his head.

He walked them back to Ian, who seemed to be unaware of the tension crackling between Bekah and the man she had introduced as "just another passenger."

The rest of the party showed up. They sat outside, beneath the star-swept sky, torches burning brightly around them. They had an unobstructed view of Waikiki Beach, just a few steps away.

Scott shook his head. "What a night," he said. "This really is Paradise."

Bekah's hands were shaking. She unfolded her heavy linen napkin and laid it across her lap, clenching her hands together underneath it. Her mother had arranged the seating, and she had placed her daughter between Ian and "our guest"— Scott. Bekah had no idea how she was going to hold up through dinner.

Ian was humiliating her. *And he doesn't even realize it. He's almost completely ignoring me. He's not acting at all like a man whose sweetheart's been gone almost a year. And Scott knows it.*

But if he had anything to say about it, he respected her situation.

Then, as pineapple ice cream and macaroons were served, he said, with all apparent innocence, "Miss Martin, are you enrolling in the nurses' emergency care course the Army is holding at Tripler?"

Bekah almost choked on her pineapple ice cream. "The *what?*"

"Yeah," Scott said, although Bekah could see a mischievous smile playing over his features. "You hear about it, Doctor Martin?"

"Actually, I have," Bekah's father said as he sipped his coffee. "In fact, I'm sending one of my nurses to it. I hadn't thought of it for Bekah, but that's a marvelous idea. Especially if we need to prepare for the worst."

"What about . . . home?" Bekah demanded. "And I have a wedding to get ready for." She glanced at Ian, but he was reaching for the sugar bowl on the table. *Doesn't he care?*

"Bekah's right," Mrs. MacLaughlin said. "We have fittings and all kinds of things to organize."

"It runs Mondays through Fridays," her father continued, thinking it over. "It only lasts a couple of weeks, and it starts next week."

Bekah could tell that her father was hoping she'd do it. She ticked her glance to her aunt, who was looking at Scott, a bemused smile on her lips.

"Oh, she can't do that to Ian," Bekah's mother said. "He hasn't seen her in a year."

Ian stopped stirring his sugar into his coffee. "We'd have a week, right?" he said slowly. "And then it's just Monday through Friday?"

Bekah sagged. "Okay," she said softly.

As the older people sipped their coffee, Mari suggested the four young people take a walk around the grounds. Bekah found herself arm in arm with Mari, the two young men strolling on either side of them.

"So this is Waikiki," Scott said.

The moon hung like a large silver pearl in the black velvet sky. Palm branches cut lacy silhouettes across it like a filigree setting. Flowers blossomed everywhere, and the thick, heady perfumes permeated Bekah's hair and clothes. Mari was wearing something spicy, and the odors of the hotel restaurant combined with the clean, salty fragrance of the nearby beach.

"They should bottle this," Scott said aloud. "Call it 'Aloha Nights' or something."

Bekah couldn't help smiling in his direction. As

had happened a few times now, they were on the exact same wavelength.

"How did you hear of the nurses' training course?" she asked him.

He shrugged. "I got my sources. People from New York are resourceful."

Ian said, "I've heard that New York is grubby and filled with foreigners."

"Ian," Bekah remonstrated.

"Oh, it is," Scott assured him. "Kind of like Hawaii, only minus the grubby part."

Looking pained, Ian nodded. "Too many foreigners. I'll be glad when everybody leaves us in peace."

"We're not exactly natives," Bekah said gently.

"Well, *you're* newcomers," Ian said. "But my people have been here since the 1800s."

"My parents still speak Japanese," Mari said stiffly. "I guess that makes us foreigners."

Bekah thought about Mrs. Kaliskis and how anxious she had been that people might think she was a Communist. How had Mari fared, being of Japanese descent, when the men stationed on the island might go to war with Japan any day?

Scott shook his head. "The part about all us outsiders going ain't gonna happen, Jackson. War's on the way."

"That's what you military guys want, isn't it?" Ian asked, raising his chin in a challenging gesture.

Mari shot Bekah a nervous glance, and Bekah tugged on Ian's sleeve.

Scott opened his mouth to say something in reply, but Bekah held up her hand.

"Let's leave off talk of the war for now, okay?" she asked. "I just got home."

"Yeah, I gotta find Jimmy anyway." Scott shook his head. "That guy can get into more trouble . . ."

He said to Bekah, "Welcome home, Miss Martin. Mr. MacLaughlin." He bowed to Mari and said, "*Oyasuminasai*, Fujisaki-san."

Mari bowed back. "*Sumimasen*, DeAngelo-san. *Oyasuminasai*."

Scott moved off from the group and walked toward a sign that read, "Employees Only."

"I like him," Mari said. "He's a real glamour puss." She lowered her voice and glanced at Ian, who was walking away from them. "Gosh, Bekah, weren't you even tempted?"

"Heck, no. I'm engaged." Her voice almost cracked, but she kept herself under control. She caught up with Ian and slid her hand underneath his top arm and found his hand. Pulling gently, she made him lower it until they were holding hands. She swung his arm as they walked along.

"Will you miss me while I'm taking the nurses' course?" she asked sweetly.

"Mmm-hmm." He smiled at her. "Pele's getting fat. She needs you to ride her."

"Your dad thinks Mybabytoo fathered a litter of puppies," Mari added. "Down Wailuku. Mr. Ling's trying to find homes for them."

"Oh, I've been homesick," Bekah said, stretching. "It'll be so good to be home at last." She yawned. "Excuse me."

Mari said, "You've had such a long day, Bekah. Maybe we should turn in."

They returned to the lobby and met up with their parents. Everyone said their good nights. There were a few easygoing jokes about keeping an eye on the engaged couple—"No sneaking across the hall, now!"—that mildly shocked Bekah's mother, it was clear. But the Martins took it all with good grace.

Ian gave her a soft kiss in front of everyone, eliciting a few more teasing remarks about sneaking around in the dead of night. He said, "I'm glad you're home." Then he walked off with his parents.

Soon Bekah and Mari were alone in their room. It was lovely, decorated Hawaiian-style, with *tapa* cloths and batiks and a profusion of birds of paradise on the open-air *lanai*.

Mari climbed into mauve silk pajamas, while Bekah opted for one of her new lacy nightgowns from an exclusive shop on Union Square. As Mari brushed her hair before the dressing-table mirror, Bekah walked to the *lanai*. It hung over the lower section of the hotel.

She reached behind her head and pulled up her hair, then let it tumble over her shoulders as she gazed up at the moon. The stars were brilliant. The ocean gently brushed against the sand.

He's there.

Down on the beach, Scott was watching her. He raised his hand to his lips and blew her a good-night kiss.

Bekah couldn't stop herself.

She blew one in return.

He stood quietly, simply gazing up at her.

"Bekah? Where'd you get this twin set?" Mari called. "It's dreamy!"

Bekah moved reluctantly back into the room. "Union Square," she murmured.

"You've got to tell me everything," Mari said. "Oh, I envy you, Bekah! I'd give anything to go to the mainland."

"It was nice," Bekah said, distracted.

"*Nice.* How descriptive."

"I'm tired, Mari. I'll tell you all about it tomorrow. Promise."

"All right." Mari flopped onto her bed and rolled over. "If you snore, I will shoot you," she announced.

"I never snore," Bekah retorted, affronted.

"I'll bet Ian does." Mari giggled. "You'll have to tell me."

"*Mari.*"

"G'night."

Bekah got into bed and stared up at the ceiling fan as it rotated slowly. The fresh air wafted through the open window and the *lanai* door. Her heart was thudding so loudly that she could hear it in her ears.

After a short time, Mari's breathing grew soft and shallow. She was asleep.

Bekah got up and tiptoed to the *lanai*.

Scott was still there.

Before she could stop herself, she put on her robe and slippers and crept into the hall. She minced down the stairs. There was no one at the front desk as she tiptoed past, then took the back entrance, which led to the beach.

She ran to him. He gathered her up in his arms and held her close. They kissed.

"What am I doing?" she whispered as he covered her face with kisses.

"Don't think," he ordered her. "Don't think."

"This is wrong."

"This is as right as it gets," he countered. He took her palm and flattened her fingers over his chest. "Hear my heart? It's beating out an S.O.S."

She tapped out the Morse code with her finger. He smiled. "You know code."

She tapped out S-C-O-T-T.

He covered her upper chest, his fingertips brushing the V of skin exposed by her robe, and tapped out R-E-B-E-K-A-H D-E-A-N-G-E-L-O.

She caught her breath and tried to pull her hand away.

"Uh-uh," he said. He kept her hand pressed against his chest. "Guess who told me about the nurses' training course."

She shrugged.

"Your aunt."

"*What?*"

He tapped Y-E-S.

"Auntie!" she cried, then covered her mouth. Whispering, she said, "I'm shocked at her."

"She loves you. She wants you to be happy."

Bekah tried again to pull her hand away. Again, he held it tightly.

"This isn't the Middle Ages, you know. No one's going to cast you out of the village if you break your 'betrothal.' And I don't know how to break it to you, but Ian's not in love with you." He flashed a crooked grin at her. "In case that had escaped your notice."

"He's the thoughtful, pensive type," she retorted.

"He's your shield. You're scared to love me." He looked her straight in the eye. "You're scared I'm going to die in the war."

"Scott," she said, gasping.

"You're even afraid to say it. To think it." He pulled her close. "I can't guarantee anything, Bekah. I can't promise I won't die. Hell, a shark could crawl out of the ocean right now and chew me up."

She managed a smile. "Sharks can't crawl."

"And pigs can't fly. But bullets . . ." He held out his hands. "We could all die in this war. Does that mean we stop living until it's over? Live without feeling, postponing everything? Not me."

He kissed her hard.

She kissed him back.

And then the memory of the fire shot through her, hard and real and white-hot; she saw David reaching out to her, one last time, and the flames shooting up —

"I saw him burned alive," she wailed. "I saw it all!"

She jerked herself away from Scott and ran back into the hotel.

The nightmares, when sleep came, were horrible. David was burning. His hands were scorched and blistered, and he reached for her, whispering, "You can't love anyone else, Bekah. Only me. Only me."

Mari finally woke her up. She turned on the lights and said, in a haggard, sleepy voice, "I take it all back. Please snore, Bekah. I beg of you."

It was like a strange dream to go home the next day. As the MacLaughlin yacht pulled up to the

Maui dock, Bekah's spirit soared like the sea gulls wheeling across the brilliant sunset. Familiar faces waited to greet her: a few old Maui girlfriends, the MacLaughlin staff, and some of Dr. Martin's nurses from Kula Sanatorium. They all put fresh rainbow *leis* of orchids, *lokelani*, and mums over her head and kissed her happily.

"So, you're going to start helping us, yes?" asked Nurse Sarmiento, as the group walked to the waiting MacLaughlin cars. "Believe me, we could use an extra pair of hands at Kula these days."

Nurse Delgado nodded in assent. "Every time we try to recruit a new nurse, she winds up joining the Army Nurses Corps. It's not fair."

"I'm going to go to Tripler for the emergency training course," Bekah told them.

The two nurses groaned in unison.

"No way you'll be back," Nurse Delgado said. "They'll figure out some way to make you stay. Dangle money at you. Or a fancy title. All the nurses are lieutenants."

"Ladies, please," Paul Martin said, chuckling. "First of all, Bekah's not an R.N., and only R.N.'s are lieutenants. And secondly, she's engaged, remember? She's not likely to stay on another island for long while her fiancé's over here growing cane."

"Okay, so, *mo bettah?*" Bekah teased as she climbed into the luxurious De Soto and made room as Ian squeezed in beside her. "I told 'em, didn't I?" she asked her fiancé.

He settled his plantation hat in his lap. His scarred side was away from her, and she wondered if he had planned it that way. She didn't remember his being so sensitive about it before. She wondered what had happened to him in her absence to make him self-conscious of it.

"I'm not growing much cane," he said flatly. "I've told you that. So don't be shocked."

"Of course I won't."

But as they drove through the familiar land-scape, as beach sand gave way to the flat plains, Bekah grew quiet. On the far outskirts of the plan-tation, the devastation the fire had caused was still visible from the road. With ten months gone by, she would have expected it all to have regrown with lush, tropical vegetation, if not cultivated cane fields. The wooden fences were still scorched and partially missing.

"This must be difficult for you," she said in a whisper. "Letting me see this."

He looked at her blankly. "Why should it be? You're part of the family. We can sell this to a big company, make a lot of money."

"But . . ." She hesitated. "This is your heritage."

"Up in smoke," he bit off.

The cars stopped at the front steps of their house, untouched and beautiful. Mrs. MacLaughlin and Bekah's mother, who had ridden in the other car, approached Bekah's car and gestured for her to join them. Bekah obeyed, having to climb over Ian, who shied away from the contact.

Mrs. MacLaughlin took Bekah's hands in her own. "Now that you're here . . ." She smiled sadly. "We have new hope that our family will go on. I know you're exactly what we all need."

Bekah licked her lips nervously. "I'll try."

Mrs. MacLaughlin's eyes welled. "Do you want to visit David's grave, dear?" When Bekah started to look over her shoulder at Ian, his mother said, "We discussed it beforehand. He wants you to have time alone. With David."

Bekah nodded. *"Mahalo,"* she said feelingly.

Bekah's mother stepped away, and Mrs. MacLaughlin and Bekah walked hand in hand to the family cemetery, at a distance behind the house. Headstones dating all the way back to the original missionaries stood in the grassy plot.

Bekah spotted the familiar stone, and her throat grew tight. David's monument was of an angel, holding her hands toward heaven.

DAVID ANDREW MACLAUGHLIN, 1918-1940, his stone read. *BELOVED SON AND BROTHER. REST IN PEACE.*

"I'll leave you for a moment," Mrs. MacLaughlin said, kissing Bekah's cheek. "Take all the time you want."

Tears spilled down Bekah's face. She balled her fists and pressed her hands tightly against her abdomen. Her lips trembled.

"Oh, David," she whispered. "David, I'm home. I miss you so much. Everyone does. Ian's bitter, and I don't know if he loves me at all. I don't know if I . . . can do this. I'm in love again, David. But it's not with Ian. I will never be in love with Ian."

She let out a single deep sob. Then she crossed her hands over her mouth.

I will never say that to anyone, she vowed. *I will never let anyone know.*

She took off all her *leis* and draped them over the head of David's angel. Then she touched her hand to her lips and pressed them against David's name.

In Morse code, she tapped out, A-L-O-H-A.

She turned and walked to Mrs. MacLaughlin, who was wiping her eyes with a handkerchief.

"I'm sure he's happy to know you're coming home to stay," she said. "He knows what a hole he left. And here you are, to fill it."

She put her arm around Bekah, and the two women trudged slowly back to the others. Bekah felt weighted down, as if they were carrying David's casket with them.

Will it grow lighter as time goes on? Bekah wondered.

The Martins and the MacLaughlins had dinner together, and afterward, Bekah went with her parents to their weekend house. She and Ian hadn't spent one moment alone together, and he didn't seem inclined to push for one.

Her mind returned again and again to the night before, to Scott's kisses and his caresses. Ian's lack of interest wounded her.

He won't even know I'm unhappy, she realized. *He'll never pay that much attention to me.*

Her old room seemed small and simple after the luxury of her aunt's San Francisco mansion. Mybabytoo was waiting for her, as always, and he curled up at the foot of her narrow bed when she crawled in to go to sleep.

She smiled wistfully at the magazine pictures of Errol Flynn she had cut out. Mari had written on one, *Ha-cha-cha!* with little hearts and flowers around the words. There was her collection of seashells and her prized ashtray from the Maui Country Fair. David had won it for her at a booth.

In the morning, there were pancakes and fresh pineapple for breakfast. Her mother was bustling around the small house, which was little more than a bungalow but a luxury for a physician, who, after all, didn't make that large a salary. Aunt Miriam kept insulting her without realizing it, exclaiming over how "quaint" and "sweet" everything was, until her sister-in-law was grinding her teeth.

Then Ian came by unannounced after breakfast, riding Duke and trailing Pele. Bekah leaped onto the horse, and the two rode away, Ian cantering, Bekah galloping for all she was worth.

Finally, near a stream, she dismounted and sat on a rock, waiting for Ian. She tickled her palm with a soft fern, finding comfort in the natural splendor around her.

Ian dismounted and came up beside her. She smiled pleasantly at him.

He said, "I don't want to marry you, Bekah."

Even though she had known it, it was still a blow. And even though it was what she wanted, it still hurt. Her eyes filled with tears, and she nodded, playing absently with the fern.

"It's no good. It's just . . . I like you. But . . . I *like* you." He held out his hands. "I don't get why I don't love you. More," he amended. "As much as you should be loved. But I just don't *feel* it."

"I know," she whispered. She shaded her eyes as she searched his face. "I'm grateful to you. It would have been easier just to marry me, wouldn't it?"

He nodded. "A lot easier, Rebekah. But you deserve better." He leaned over and kissed her very softly. "I hope you find it."

"Thank you." She put her arms around him. They hugged in silence.

Then they mounted their horses and rode back to the Martin homestead. Bekah kissed Pele on the forehead.

"I'll miss you, girl," she said.

"You can ride her whenever you want." He cleared his throat. "I'll tell my parents."

She touched his foot. "I would have made a good wife."

"Don't I know it." He grinned at her. "*Mo bettah* stay friends."

"*Mo bettah.*"

She went inside the house. Her aunt looked up from a letter she was writing, one of a stack.

"We're not getting married," Bekah announced.

Aunt Miriam looked a little sad, and then she said, "And you're due back on Oahu in a few days to begin your training."

"Don't even think it," Bekah said.

Her aunt pantomimed zipping her mouth shut and throwing away the key.

With her mother and father still reeling in shock at the reversal in the marriage plans, Bekah took a commercial ship back to Oahu with her aunt. Aunt Miriam had decided to stay at the Royal Hawaiian so that Bekah could spend her weekends with her. During the week, Bekah was required to stay at the nurses' quarters at Fort Shafter, where the wooden Army hospital was located.

Her instructor was Nurse Lt. Carson, career Army, a bit coarse and slightly weathered from the sun. She took an immediate liking to Bekah, which increased to respect when she discovered that

Bekah's father was a medical doctor. Everyone bustled about in starched white uniforms with white stockings and white shoes, and Bekah even got to wear a nurse's cap, even though she wasn't an R.N.

Soon she was learning how to treat severe wounds such as first-degree burns and deep cuts. She was allowed to accompany the physicians on their rounds of patients—all military men—who were delighted to see the six pretty young nurses of Bekah's class grouped around their beds.

"If we go to war, you'll see more than cuts and bruises," Lt. Carson warned her students. "We have fewer than five hundred beds. We'll have to set up triage with Queen's Hospital and the naval hospital on the base."

Bekah thought of Scott. She hadn't contacted him, but neither had he attempted to contact her. She was devastated. Apparently, she had been nothing more than one of his "girls in every port."

"Martin, tell me, have you thought of signing up?" Lt. Carson asked Bekah as the two of them were having Cokes in the nurses' lounge. It was six at night but warm enough in the hospital to melt the cubes of butter on the tables in the medical staff dining room. All the windows were open, and the ceiling fans were turning lazily. "It would suit you perfectly."

Bekah felt both panicky and thrilled. Until

recently, she had thought her life was all planned out. Now, there were no boundaries or limits. It was scary.

"Maybe I will."

"I could put in a word for you. We could use you. You're not an R.N., but I'm certain we could work something out."

"I'll think about it," Bekah said. "My parents live here, and . . ."

"I understand. You've got your father's work at Kula to consider." She chuckled. "We keep stealing his nurses."

Bekah smiled at her. "Yes, you do."

Lt. Carson clapped her hands together.

"Well, Nurse Martin, I think you're ready for the big time. How about assisting in an operating room?"

"Now?" she asked, startled.

The older woman took a swig of her Coke. "Next week will do."

This was a promotion, and Bekah knew it. None of the trainees had been permitted to assist in the O.R. as yet. "You think so?" Bekah asked excitedly.

"Absolutely. Do you have a strong stomach?"

Bekah nodded. "I got to observe in San Francisco."

"Even better."

Lt. Carson set down her Coke and cracked her knuckles. The tips of her fingers were yellow from heavy smoking. "I'm afraid we're going to have a lot of need for surgically trained nurses once we enter the war. It's not going to be pretty."

Bekah bit her lower lip. All the military people seemed positive that the war was coming very soon. They just didn't know when.

Just then, another nurse poked her head in. "Bekah?" she asked. "There's a young man asking to see you."

Her heart skipped a beat. *Scott!* A happy thrill skittered up her spine. She hadn't seen him since the day they'd landed.

Bekah smoothed back her hair and her starched apron, caught herself, and smiled shyly at Lt. Carson.

"Family friend," she murmured.

"Go along. You've got twenty minutes left on your dinner break." Lt. Carson picked up her Coke and took another sip. "I don't think I could get up from this couch to meet Captain Cook himself. It's too warm to move, if you ask me."

Bekah's heart pounded as she walked into the lobby area. Her white nursing shoes squeaked on the neutral tile floor, freshly polished and waxed to a sheen. She saw him framed in the long afternoon sun. Scott was wearing his tropical whites; in the weeks since they'd been in Hawaii, he'd acquired a deep tan. His hair was streaked with blond.

He turned, saw her, and smiled broadly. "Hey. How's it going?"

"Swell," she blurted, then cleared her throat. "Fine." She exhaled, not sure what to expect from him—also aware that they were on military property, where members of the armed forces did not generally hug and kiss each other. "Actually, I love my training. It's so exciting."

"You're lucky, then." He seemed awkward, too. "My ship's in worse shape than I expected."

She rocked back on her heels. "Not shipshape, huh?"

They both smiled. "Nope," he said, "not at all. She's an old heap. There's a move to decommission her, and I'm all for it. The BB-36 has had her day. She's the oldest battleship here."

"How disappointing," she said. She could barely keep her attention on the conversation. Her body was singing. Her lips were remembering the night on the beach.

Scott said, "Let's go outside. It's too close in here."

They turned to the right and walked out a side door. The lush, heady odors of flowers saturated the steamy night. Scott carried his hat under his arm, and the moonlight glinted against the crown of his head. He was so handsome it took her breath away.

Then he pulled her into his arms and kissed her

hard. It was a passionate kiss, and she answered it with every fiber of her being. He cradled the back of her head, adoring her, worshiping her, and then he laid her head against his chest. His heart was beating very fast.

"Bekah, things are heating up. The war's coming any day."

"*Some* people say that," she countered. "Some people think it will never come."

A muscle jumped in his cheek, and the pulse in his temple quickened.

"Bekah, I ain't no fancy fella. I'm a pusher. If the rules are in my way, I make different ones. And you can ask anybody in the big, overgrown city of Manhattan—I don't take no for an answer."

He looked hard at her, and her breath caught in her throat.

"Bekah, I'm going to fight in a war. I have got nothing to offer you. Except me. And I got to be straight. From where I sit, I'd be a hell of a lot better for you than that . . . that . . ."

He ran his hand through his hair. "Something happened to him, to make him not care. About himself. About life. He's sour. He doesn't love you, honey. He's just going along because it's easier."

Her mouth fell open.

"I'm not forcing myself on you. But my old man—a guy who held down two jobs, and it finally killed him way too young—he told me once, 'It's not the things in life we do that we regret. It's the things we don't do that haunt us.' "

He held out his arms. "I'm not going to be haunted by the thought that I didn't fight for you. Bekah, I love you. I want you to marry me, not that scarred-up —"

"Scott—" She pulled on her arm. He held her firm. Then he wrapped his arm around her waist and drew her against his chest.

Her body was responding to his. Her senses were racing. It took her total concentration not to melt against his long, lean frame. The pins holding her nurse's cap in place came loose, and it fell off her head. Her hair tumbled around her shoulders.

"Scott, I . . ." She licked her lips. "I'm so scared."

Just then, a corpsman approached, saluting Scott. "Ensign DeAngelo?" he queried politely. "Sir, someone's looking for you. Said his name is Jimmy. He's on the lobby phone, sir."

"Now what?" Scott muttered under his breath. He saluted the corpsman. "Thanks."

He exhaled wearily. "Our C.O.—Commanding Officer—said one more infraction and he's going to throw him in the brig."

"Be careful," Bekah blurted, touching his arm.

"I'm not going anywhere until you say yes."

She hesitated. "I need to think."

"You'll say yes."

"Let me think."

His expression was hungry, pleading. He cupped her cheek, then ran his thumb across her lips.

"Don't be scared, okay? Be brave. For me."

"I *am* scared," she whispered. "I can't help it."

"It'll be all right."

He went to get the phone.

"You can't promise that," she said to the retreating figure.

∽9∽

Tripler Hospital
December 6, 1941, 8 P.M.

"Well, I say marry him," Lt. Carson said to Bekah. "You love him, he loves you . . ." She trailed off. "So what's the problem?"

Bekah picked up another stack of charts. They were filing; she hated filing. It was make-work. She wanted to be in the O.R., where the action was.

"I was engaged before," she confessed. "My fiancé died."

"Oh. Complications."

Lt. Carson put down her pile of brown medical records and fished for a cigarette. She lit it, drew in the smoke, and exhaled through her nose. "And we're on the brink of war. I see your dilemma."

"You do?" Bekah asked gratefully.

Aunt Miriam did not. She thought Bekah was being "melodramatic." And her parents, when she had gone home for a late Thanksgiving feast, had been taken by complete surprise to learn that she was in love with their dinner companion.

"Kiddo, I'm career Army," Lt. Carson drawled. "I'm training fresh young girls to patch up fresh young boys after they get blown to bits. I can certainly understand why you'd rather marry a college professor." She took another drag on her cigarette. "Oh, yes, I see your problem."

She patted Bekah on the shoulder. "Time to pack it in, Martin. You did a good job today."

Bekah wiped her brow. "Thank you, Lieutenant. They need air-conditioning in this place. I'm going to sponge off in the ladies' room before I go to my quarters. When you're sharing with three other girls, it takes a while to get the bathroom to yourself."

Lt. Carson chuckled. "You go right ahead, Martin." She took a deep puff. "I'll put away a few more charts and look in on Private Okamura." Her face turned downward in a gentle expression of sorrow. "I'm afraid he's going to need specialing."

Bekah cocked her head. She knew the private had been seriously injured in a car accident. "What's specialing?"

Lt. Carson watched the smoke rise for a few moments.

"It's when a patient is dying," she said bluntly. She looked directly at Bekah. "We call it specialing. We treat them special."

"Oh." Bekah's stomach did a flip. "I see."

"Surely you've had patients die before."

"I've seen people die, yes, but they haven't been my patients," Bekah answered honestly, even though the effort cost her. She forced the sight of David's burned face away from her mind's eye and concentrated on what Lt. Carson was saying.

"Well, we stay with our boys when they're in trouble. We do what we can to make them comfortable."

Nothing could make David comfortable. He died in agony.

"I'm so sorry for Private Okamura," she said sincerely. "Would you like me to stay with you?"

"No, thank you, Martin. You're young. I imagine you and the other girls have something planned."

"Not really," Bekah replied. "Just studying."

Bekah had three other roommates in her billet in the nurses' quarters. One of them was like Bekah, studious and interested in medicine, while the other two were pretty fast. Between all the young unmarried military men stationed in the islands and a chance to see the movie stars at the Royal Hawaiian Hotel, working in Hawaii was a single girl's dream. With all the *luaus*, the dances, and the casual lifestyle, it was Paradise in far more ways than one.

"Just studying," Lt. Carson mused. "Oh, that's

right. You're engaged." She tamped out her cigarette. "Well, it's very nice of you to offer, Martin,
but you've done enough for one day."

The phone rang. Lt. Carson picked it up and
rattled off, "Tripler, yes?" She listened for a
moment, then said, "Yes, Ensign. She's standing
right here, as a matter of fact."

Bekah still hadn't given him an answer. As far as
she knew, he didn't know about her breakup with
Ian, either.

Why haven't I told him? she asked herself. But she
knew why: it was an easy out if she decided to say
no.

Letting out an anxious breath, Bekah took the
phone. "Hello?"

"Something's wrong with Jimmy," he told her. "I
found him down here—I'm on Hotel Street—and
he's gotten himself into another scrape. I hadda tell
the on-duty Military Police I started the fight, or
they were going to haul him in. I've got to see my
C.O. first thing in the morning."

Hotel Street. No self-respecting single girl would
find herself down there. "Why'd you do that?" she
asked, more harshly than she'd intended. "If it was
his fault—"

"Captain said if he screwed up one more time,
he was going to bust him down. I haven't got any
black marks against me, so I figured I'd take the
rap."

"How many times has it been, Scott? You can't keep doing this."

"Bekah, let's talk about it later, okay? He's hurt and some buddies already took him back to the ship. I tried to talk them out of it, but I was busy talking the M.P.'s out of hauling me in. I'm due back at the *Nevada*. Will you come out and take a look at him?"

"On your ship?" Her voice was shrill. Lt. Carson looked at her with mild curiosity and mouthed, "I'm going to Okumura." Then she left the nurses' station.

"It's not that out of line," Scott said. "We're allowed to invite nurses on board for dinner. There were a couple of them here last night, as a matter of fact."

"Dinner's over."

"Dinner and a movie. We've got *Fantasia*. Please, Bekah. I can't bring him to you. He's already on the *Nevada*. I've got a car. I'll come and get you."

"All right."

"Thank you," he said gratefully.

She hung up and stood by the phone for a moment. Then she walked down the hall in her squeaky nurse's shoes and located the ward where Private Okumura lay. The lights in the ward were off, but in the hall light, Bekah saw Lt. Carson seated next to him, speaking softly to him.

Bekah silently approached. Lt. Carson saw her and looked up.

"I'd appreciate your advice," Bekah said. "Is it . . . something that's done . . . for nurses to go out to the battleships?"

"It's done," Lt. Carson said. "Why do you ask?" She grinned. "Is this Mr. Proposal?"

"Yes," Bekah said haltingly.

"Go."

Bekah looked down at Okamura, whose face was sheened with perspiration. Lt. Carson dipped a wet cloth in a kidney-shaped bowl and pressed the cool water to Okamura's mouth. He sucked on the cloth.

"That's good, Private," she said.

"Yes . . . yes, ma'am," he gasped. His eyes rolled up toward Bekah. "Nurse?" he whispered.

Bekah drew closer. "Yes, Private?"

"I thought maybe I was dreaming you," he said with great effort.

"No. I'm here."

"You look like an angel." He fell silent. She waited for him to say more, and when he didn't, Bekah stared at him in alarm.

"You rest, Okamura. We're going to need you soon," Lt. Carson said.

"Yes, ma'am."

The older woman's eyes filled with tears. "Go to your ensign."

Bekah nodded and left the ward.

In the hall, she pressed her hand against her eyes and said a very short prayer for Private Okamura.

Shaking, she sponged off as she had planned. She sprayed herself with a little eau de cologne and ran a comb through her hair.

About fifteen minutes later, Scott pulled up to the front of the hospital. He was driving a Jeep. She was down the stairs and climbing in before he had even turned off the engine.

"Bekah." He reached out to hold her, and she melted against him.

As he pulled out and made for the main gate, he said, "I appreciate this. I would never have asked if that moron hadn't already gotten himself in so deep already."

"I need to tell you something," she said. "I . . . Ian and I broke it off."

"I know." He glanced at her. "Your aunt mentioned it to me a couple days ago. I was wondering why you hadn't told me."

She cleared her throat. "You know why."

He put his hand over hers.

They took Kamehameha Highway down to the Pearl Harbor main gate. Scott, in his uniform, was waved through.

"We're going to Bravo Pier," he said. "That's where the liberty launches put in." He checked his watch. "The nine o'clock will be here soon." He took off his cap and ran his fingers through his hair. He was agitated.

"What happened to Jimmy?"

Scott snorted with disgust and pulled the Jeep into a marked spot. Taxis were depositing other men in uniform, the majority of them sailors, and they were laughing and singing, obviously drunk.

Scott said, "He got into a knife fight over some dame. Not even some dame worth fighting over, if you know what I mean."

"I do," she said primly.

A few of the sailors started glancing in her direction. Scott scowled at them, and they turned away, snickering. Bekah heard something about "the slick chick," and her cheeks flamed.

Scott heard, too. "This is nuts. I'm not going to drag you into this," he said. "Get back in the flivver."

Just then, the *putt-putt-putt* of a motor clattered over all the dockside conversations. A small gray metal boat pulled up to the dock. Canvas tarp covered the rails all the way around, and a sailor stood in the center beside a diesel engine.

"Twenty-one-hundred-hours skiff," the sailor called. "Bound for the *Nevada*."

Bekah said, "Take me to him, Scott. I'll be all right."

He looked at her strangely. "It just occurred to

me, I'm doing the same thing I accused you of. Jimmy's pretty much thrown a monkey wrench in my life, and I keep letting him do it."

"He's hurt," Bekah pointed out.

"He's hurt," Scott agreed. "If you're sure."

"I'm sure." She smiled at him. "I think."

He took her hand and walked her to the skiff. Her presence created a stir as Scott and the pilot assisted her aboard. She was the only female. The smirks on the faces of the other passengers were humiliating, but Bekah held her head high and said nothing. Scott took her hand and gave it a squeeze.

The night smelled of diesel exhaust, oil, alcohol, and sweat. Bekah was glad for the cologne she'd sprayed on before Scott picked her up.

Soon they were heading past an astonishing expanse of gray metal—the hulls of all the battleships moored on Battleship Row. They were lined up in a double row. The names were illuminated, and as they passed the outer row, Bekah read off the names to herself: *Oklahoma*, *West Virginia*, *Vestal*, *Arizona*. And, finally, the *Nevada*.

All the ships were immense, but Scott said to her, "We're only five-hundred-eighty-three feet long," as if that were a number to scoff at. The vessel was taller than most buildings. Guns peered at them from mounts of square blocks of cement or metal. A huge structure of some kind rose from the center of the ship, and it was surrounded by guns the size of automobile tunnels, or so it seemed to Bekah. Towering high above them, twin structures were held in place by enormous tripods that vaguely resembled the cranes that were used on occasion to dredge the harbor.

The ship's vast arsenal struck terror into Bekah's heart. *What is coming?* she thought. *This war . . . surely it will destroy the entire world.*

One of the sailors began singing "Home, Sweet Home," and a few of the others joined in. By their sarcastic, off-key melody, Bekah figured they were as ashamed of their vessel as Scott was.

The launch *vroomed* to a landing platform. Bekah was glad of her flat, thick-soled nursing shoes as she surveyed the ladder she would have to climb to go aboard.

"Liberty launch requests permission to come aboard, sir," the pilot boomed, saluting.

A man walked forward on the deck of the *Nevada*, which was at the other end of the ladder. An armed sailor stood at attention to his right.

He said, "State your business, Ensign DeAngelo."

"*Fantasia*, sir," Scott said, and the others laughed.

"Very well. Permission granted."

Scott said in a low voice, "Go up before me. I'll stand beneath you so they don't try to look up your skirt."

He gestured to the officer on the deck. "He's a friend of mine. Let him help you."

She was mildly shocked, but she did as he said. The officer smiled at her and held out both his hands. "I'm the officer of the deck," he told her. "What're you doing with that Italian, anyway? He's just a bum from New York."

"Sir, she's never seen *Fantasia*, sir," Scott said with a slight tinge of irony as he came up behind her.

The two men saluted each other, and Scott walked Bekah away from the cluster of men who were getting in trouble for coming aboard intoxicated.

"Officers' country is first and second deck," he said. "Most of the senior officers are away tonight. And it just occurred to me, what were you doing working on a Saturday night?"

She moved her shoulders. "I volunteered."

They walked past the big guns, pointed ominously toward the sky. The largest ones poked from the centers of what looked to be enormous, thick bunkers. Scott explained that they were called turrets. Smaller ones were located another level up, with barriers set behind them. They were called directors. Then, in the center of the ship between the two cranelike masts was a towering structure with a wide window. He called that War-Room Central.

"We've got ten fifteen-inch guns and twelve five-inch," Scott said, gesturing at them. "We've been refitted at least twice. Heck, we were commissioned in 1916. That makes us the oldest battleship. And we're the smallest, us and the *Oklahoma*."

"It's still very impressive," she said, nearly tripping over a piece of chain so huge it could encompass a car tire. Everything seemed to be made for giants. She felt dwarfed in comparison.

"Yeah, well, tell that to Adolf," he retorted, meaning Hitler. "Or the Japanese." He glanced over his shoulder at her. "We'll get 'em, though. Once they declare war, we'll be on them like hornets."

He opened a hatch and gestured for her to follow him in. "Watch your step," he said, pointing to the foot-high lip at the bottom of the doorway.

"Another ladder, sorry," he announced. He took it first. She followed after. When they got to the bottom, she saw a sign with fierce-looking sailors carrying bayonets that read, *THEY'RE READY. ARE YOU?*

He led her down a tight, narrow corridor and then another. He rapped once, then opened the cabin door.

A man dressed in tropical whites was seated on a pull-out rack. He was hunched over another man, this one lying on his back and groaning. It was Jimmy Toombs.

The man who had been watching over Jimmy slumped when he saw Scott.

"Jeez, DeAngelo, where you been?"

"Sorry." Scott peered at Jimmy. "How is he?"

"What you see, that's how he is." The man checked his watch. "I'm going ashore."

"Have a good time. Stay out of trouble," Scott said without looking at the man. "And thanks for keeping an eye on him."

The man nodded at Bekah and said, "Ma'am." Then he squeezed past her and headed down the corridor.

She entered the cramped cabin. Besides the pull-out racks, there were two lockers and a tiny desk with a lamp on it. That was all . . . except for a pinup of a scantily clad Hawaiian girl posing on the beach.

"Sorry about that," Scott said, removing it from the wall.

Bekah was mildly amused, and touched by his consideration, as she bent over Jimmy. She wished she'd thought to grab a stethoscope. Instead, she pinched his wrist and kept track of his pulse on her nurse's watch. Next, she checked his pupils, fanning the sharp odor of alcohol away as best she could.

"Hey, Miss Martin," Jimmy said. "It's my stomach."

Several white blankets were laid across his flat torso. She carefully peeled them away. The last one was wet with his blood. His stomach was criss-crossed with cuts, some fairly deep. The flesh sur-rounding them was inflamed. His forehead was as hot as Private Okamura's had been.

"What about your medics on board?" Bekah asked Scott.

"No," Jimmy moaned. "Please."

She made a face. Scott shrugged.

"All right. Get me some sterile gauze and some kind of antiseptic," she ordered, again chastising herself for not coming prepared.

Scott left the cabin. Jimmy groaned, and she snapped at him, "You stop drinking, do you under-stand me? If you get him in trouble, I'll never for-give you."

"I'm trying," he whispered, in obvious pain.

She cleaned and dressed his wounds, then set about bringing down his fever with cold com-presses while Scott looked on. After a time, he said, "I should take you back, Bekah. You've done a swell job."

"I want to make sure his fever's down," she insisted. "Then we'll go."

The next thing she knew, she jerked awake. She was lying in the other bunk, facing the wall. Scott was curled around her, breathing shallowly. Her back was pressed against his chest, and his left arm was holding her against him. His breathing teased and tantalized her ear. The side of his face was warm against hers, the night's stubbly growth a reminder that he was a man.

And that she was a woman.

"Scott?" she whispered fiercely.

"You fell asleep. I tried to wake you, but you told me it wasn't time for school yet. And you called me Mom."

Her cheeks grew warm. "You're making that up."

He chuckled under his breath. "Nope."

Yawning, she squinted at her watch. "What time is it?"

"I think it's three. Maybe four. I let you sleep while I stood my watch."

She bolted upright. "Are you out of your mind? I can't stay here all night." She lowered her voice. "I'll be tossed out of the program—not to mention my family—and you'll be court-martialed. At least."

"Yeah. I thought about that."

She moved to Jimmy and felt his forehead. It was cool, and he was sleeping peacefully. That was something, at least.

Scott looked contrite. "But there are no more skiffs until sunup. So we might as well get comfortable."

"What?" She batted at him. "Scott!" she whispered. "I can't stay here, in bed with you!"

He caught her wrists and gently pulled her

toward him. "Nothing will happen, Bekah. I swear it."

His lips covered hers with a kiss. His mouth was warm and gentle, and she knew she could stop him any time she chose to.

"Nothing will happen," she said slowly. She began to tremble.

"Bekah, don't go," he said urgently. "Why are you so afraid of me?"

"I'm not afraid of you," she insisted, her voice trembling. "I'm not."

He rolled to one side, lying half on her body, and gathered her hair in his hands. He cradled the back of her head in his hand and whispered, "What happened on Maui, Bekah? What's going on?"

She licked her lips. "Nothing that concerns you."

"Everything about you concerns me."

She closed her eyes. "I can't. I've never told anyone."

"You can tell me." His dark brown eyes filled her field of vision. And yet she could still see the flames of the cane field rising behind them . . . or was there desire for Scott DeAngelo, burning deep inside?

She told the story, painfully, slowly.

"Then I just ran," she confessed brokenly. "David was burning to death, and I went crazy. I didn't see Ian until I barreled into him. I knocked him over, and he fell into a patch of burning cane.

You saw his face." She whimpered. "I did that to him."

"Ah, Bekah," he said, gathering her up against him. "Stop blaming yourself. You didn't cause any of that. You didn't."

"I can't go through that again."

There was a long silence. Then Scott said, "Then you can't love, Bekah. Because I can't protect you from that kind of grief. No one can."

There was a finality about his words that made her cold.

"We're parting," she said, stunned.

He took a breath and stood. Helping her up, he said, "I'm taking you to the O.O.D. They'll find somewhere for you to sleep until the morning liberty launch at eight."

∽10∽

Pearl Harbor
December 7, 1941, 5 A.M.

True to his word, Scott took the officer of the deck aside and quietly explained the situation at hand. Bekah stood by, mortified and grief-stricken, but she managed to maintain her composure.

The O.O.D. was stern with Scott but gentle with Bekah. He said, "Miss, I apologize on behalf of the crew. You should not have been put through this."

She lowered her head. "Thank you."

"Ensign DeAngelo will escort you to my quarters," he told her. "My bunkmate's ashore. You'll be alone until the liberty launch debarks at eight this morning."

She nodded.

Scott guided her back down the ladder and down another warren of passageways. He pushed open a door and showed her in.

They looked at each other. He broke away first, turning silently and leaving her alone.

She fell asleep at once, too tired to feel anything.

The ship was screaming. Bells ringing, klaxon sounding.

"General quarters! This is no drill!"

The door burst open. A man Bekah had never seen before grabbed her hand and yanked her out of bed. He dragged her out of the cabin and down the passage that led to his cabin. The ship shook violently, throwing them both against the bulkhead. Debris tumbled down on their shoulders. Bekah's head rang from the thundering noises, and she couldn't tell if she screamed aloud or only in her head.

"What's going on? What's happening?" she cried.

"We're being attacked! Pearl Harbor's being attacked!"

Explosions sounded all around them, and then the ship shook so hard Bekah was certain it was coming apart. Someone screamed, "We've been torpedoed! Taking on water!"

"Don't panic!" the man shouted.

Wordlessly, she nodded. She couldn't feel anything. She could barely register what he was saying, the noise was so deafening.

They headed up the ladder, men shouting at

them both to hurry up. Her nurse's cap flew off, to be trampled by what seemed like a hundred feet.

"General quarters! This is no drill!" came the shout again. A horn was blaring. A cascade of huge explosions buffeted Bekah's entire body.

The man pulled her out onto the wooden deck just as a plane overhead strafed the deck. Dozens, hundreds of splinters shot into Bekah's ankles. She cried out and whirled around in a circle as the man let go of her and collapsed on the deck.

She fell to her knees beside him. A thick pool of blood fanned out from beneath him. *So much. Too much.*

She checked his pulse. He was dead.

Men were standing behind each of the massive guns and firing at the planes flying dangerously close. Other men worked machine guns, some standing in plain view of the planes, which had large red circles on their sides.

Japanese.

The Japanese were attacking Pearl Harbor!

Someone slammed into her, throwing her face-down on the deck. Then his full weight landed on top of her. She grunted and tried to push him off, then felt his body jerking as bullets shot into him.

She fought and flailed, and finally she rolled out from under the man. He, too, was dead.

A man raced past her, shouting, "Boilers!" She didn't have time to respond before the man had dashed away, bound for his duty station.

Rising up on her elbows, Bekah looked around at the chaos as men poured across the deck. She slid toward the center of the vessel. The ship was listing.

"Hey," said a man whose face was covered with black oil. He bent down and picked her up, setting her on her feet. He stationed himself in front of her, his back to her, and wrapped her arms around his waist. "Stick to me like glue, all right?"

He ran. Aerial machine-gun fire struck either side of them; the man pushed her away, and she fell to her knees, crouching low and shielding her head. Smoke poured over her like an ocean wave. She gagged, coughing hard, then fell onto her hands and knees and tried to stand.

Her savior was dead.

A screaming man raced toward her. His left arm was on fire. She knew he was feeding the flames by running, so she barreled into him, knocking him to the deck and covering the flames with her own body. The pain was excruciating. The man kept shrieking, batting at her in panic. The stench of burned flesh and scorched cotton filled her nose, and she began to cough and gag.

Someone threw a pail of water on them both. When she looked up, whoever had saved her life had moved on.

"We've got to get under way!" shouted a man in the tatters of a white uniform. "Come on! Where's the quartermaster?"

Then one of the Japanese planes started screaming toward the ship. The *Nevada*'s guns swiveled toward it. Men on the deck aimed machine guns straight at it; one sailor was hit and crumpled in a heap.

The plane exploded into an enormous fireball; like a comet, it plummeted into the ocean.

The cheer that rose up was deafening. "We got it!" a man bellowed in Bekah's ear. His bloody spittle hit the side of her cheek. Then he grabbed her and kissed her, smearing her mouth with blood. "We got one of them!"

As the cheering rose, Bekah became aware that there were no more planes in the air. Was it over?

As she watched the skies, something caught her eye. It was Scott, standing behind one of the smaller guns. Blood was running into his eyes.

"Scott!" she screamed, racing for him.

"Get down! Get away!" he shouted.

Then the planes came again, flying so low Bekah could see the smile on the face of the lead pilot. She wished she had a gun, a rock, anything to hit him with.

There was an enormous explosion, and she screamed. Debris flew up into the air, then cascaded back down toward the deck. It was a miracle that nothing hit her.

Then Scott was beside her, gasping, saying, "Oh, Bekah, forgive me for dragging you out here."

There was another explosion. The force knocked her backward; she tumbled end over end, shrieking, and when she finally ran into something on the deck, she thought every bone in her body had been shattered.

She wiped the dirt and blood from her eyes and saw that Scott had half fallen into the hole that had been blasted into the deck.

He was on fire.

She tried to cry out, but there was no sound in her throat. She fought her way to him, elbow over elbow, watching the flames encircling his chest. She dug into the splintered deck, leaving trails of blood.

She reached him and threw herself over his body. The flames burned her, but she didn't care. All she knew was that it was happening again. David was dying again . . .

Then she realized that she was lapsing into unconsciousness, and no one knew that Scott was up here, terribly wounded. Blood streamed from beneath him as he lay facedown. She looked around. Men were lying everywhere, wounded, their guns silent. The deck was sticky with their blood. The carnage was unspeakable.

She dragged herself to the hole and saw sailors below in knee-high water, working on some kind of machinery.

"Help," she rasped, but no one looked up. "Help."

Her voice was too weak. No one would hear her in time. Scott would die.

She saw a revolver in a man's outstretched hand and reached for it. She had to pry his dead fingers from it, but she managed it.

She slammed it down on the deck: *Dit-dit-dit-da-da-dit-dit-dit.*

S.O.S.

She did it again. And again. And again.

And suddenly, someone was coming up and taking the gun from her and shouting, "Medics!"

And someone else was screaming, "The *Arizona's* dead!"

They steamed down the center of the harbor, smoke covering them like a blanket.

"It's the *Pennsylvania,* hiding us!" someone cheered.

Huge geysers of water sprayed the deck, smashing down like bombs themselves. Bekah was soaked. Blood and soot caked her uniform. She crawled along the deck, coming upon a man with a severe chest wound. He was gasping for breath.

"Mom," he whispered. "Mom."

"Here," she managed. She reached down and tore at her hem. Her dress was little more than rags. She realized her right hand was bleeding, the blood splashing with the sea water on the deck. The deck was covered with bits of twisted metal and debris.

Once she had pulled about a yard of fabric off her body, she hesitated. The man was bleeding so badly; what could she hope to accomplish?

But he was looking up at her, staring at her. His mouth worked, but he couldn't speak.

"This will help," she assured him, although it wouldn't. She pressed the fabric against his chest, felt her fist go deep, and stuffed the material into the gaping hole in his chest.

The useless gesture seemed to relieve him. Something had been done to help him, or so he thought.

"It's all right," she said as calmly as she could. "You're going to be fine."

His glazed eyes told her he was dead.

She had no time to mourn him. As she crawled on, she came upon another man, choking on his own blood. All she could do was grab hold of his wrists and pull him to a sitting position, then scoot around and press against his back with her own, forcing him not to flop forward. She heard him cough, heard him gurgle and begin to breathe again. He was no longer choking.

She realized she couldn't move, or he might suffer the same predicament all over again. So she sat on the deck, feet outstretched, pushing with all her might against the heavy, limp man.

A fresh burst of machine-gun fire slammed into the deck just inches from her leg. She cried out but did not leave her post. She had no idea if what she was doing would keep the man alive, but it was the only thing she could think of to do.

Then she looked up and saw that part of the conning tower was coming apart and teetered directly above her. If she didn't move, she would be crushed to death.

But I can't move him, she thought, *and there's a chance it won't fall.*

Fires blazed around her. The anti-aircraft guns boomed and rattled her teeth and her bones. Her ears rang, and then she heard nothing.

I've gone deaf, she thought.

Someone found her, wrapped her in a blanket, and took her to the pilothouse. The mood was jubilant. Of all the battleships, only the *Nevada* had managed to get under way. She was making for the open waters, breaching like a dolphin. The gunners of the other ships in the harbor, crippled and dying as they were, shot blasts over the masts of the brave *Nevada* to provide a smokescreen. The Japanese planes could not locate their target, the only vessel to escape the surprise attack.

But the poor ship was burning. It had been bombed numerous times. There were casualties everywhere. Brave men refusing to leave their posts, brave men blown overboard trying to secure the ship as she listed and struggled and began to sink.

The hull of the ship screeched and shuddered as finally, the great *Nevada* was beached. Fresh faces scrambled across the deck—a rescue crew!—and a man in a helmet and a white uniform bent over Bekah.

"Please, ma'am, I'll get you lowered down in a stretcher," he told her.

"No. No time," she said.

She took one last look at the smoking hulk, still scanning for Scott, and forced herself not to cry. There would be plenty of time for that later.

"I can't go yet," she said. "I have to look for someone."

"Ma'am, rescue crews are searching the ship for survivors. It would help us more if you'd come ashore."

"No, I . . ."

They took her to Tripler. She was wounded, but it was nothing compared with the other casualties that came in. Every bed was full; some men lay on the floor, others on naked bedsprings. As she was sutured up, she watched a man bleed so much that his blood soaked the mattress and dripped on the floor.

"Please," she whispered, "let him be okay."

At her own insistence, she got a crutch and a cup of coffee, in that order. Men with more severe wounds than hers were helping out; patients with bandages wrapped around their chests inched along from bed to bed, doing what they could.

Unfortunately, there wasn't much that could be done. Supplies trickled in, but in the beginning, all she and the others could get their hands on were gauze squares and some sulfa drugs. Not one nurse in the five wards Bekah worked in could commandeer so much as a pair of scissors. She watched helplessly as men who might have lived did not.

Someone brought in sandwiches; half an hour later, Bekah couldn't remember if she'd eaten. Each time a new patient was admitted, she felt her heart stop, wondering if it was Scott. She had no idea where he was, what he was doing. The last time she had seen him was in the springhole, surrounded by fire.

Night fell—it seemed so odd to Bekah that the world still turned—and it occurred to her that back in San Francisco, Peter Contner was probably glued to his radio, listening in amazement to what had happened. She wondered if his thoughts would turn to her and Aunt Miriam. But of course they would; he would wonder about her family, too. As she was doing.

Several doctors had driven in from different parts of the islands, but they were afraid to leave the security of the hospital because the guards were shooting on sight. One of them sat for a moment with Bekah, examining her leg, which was causing her a lot of pain.

He said, "It's the strangest thing. I was at a lecture this morning at Mabel Smythe Memorial. Dr. Moorhead opened his lecture with a quote from St. Matthew: 'Be ye also ready, for in the hour that ye know not, the Son of Man cometh.' " He smiled at her wearily. "At least the sons of the Rising Sun cometh."

Bekah had no idea how much time had passed, but when she opened her eyes again, she was dozing propped up against a wall in a hallway, and Aunt Miriam was standing beside Lt. Carson.

Bekah said, "Am I dreaming?"

"Your father called some of his doctor friends over here," Aunt Miriam said. "They offered medical supplies. I helped round them up."

"Twenty-three-skidoo," Bekah said faintly.

Aunt Miriam glanced at Lt. Carson. The woman wrapped her hands around Bekah's upper arms.

"I need you to be brave," she said. "It's your young man."

"Oh, my God!" Bekah wailed. "No!"

"He's not dead," Lt. Carson said quickly. "Not yet. A shipmate of his gave his life to give him a chance. Someone named Jimmy."

"Oh," Bekah groaned. "Oh, no."

Lt. Carson took a deep breath. "He's bad off, child."

"Take me to him, take me to him," she pleaded.

Aunt Miriam and Lt. Carson each took one of her arms. Bekah cried out with pain as she tried to step on her right foot. Lt. Carson said, "I think it's broken. We don't have any splints. We were so unprepared, for all our worrying."

"I don't care," Bekah said. "I don't even feel it."

Determinedly, she dragged herself forward through the semidarkness. The two women assisted her. All but the most essential lights were off. There was black paper on the windows. The hospital was like a place of death.

They carried her into a room that reeked of burned flesh. Bekah gagged and tried to turn back.

"No, honey," Aunt Miriam whispered.

She saw the still, bandaged form and cried out. Then she saw the priest standing beside Scott's bed and began shaking her head.

"No, please," she begged. "Don't let him die."

The priest sighed. "That is in God's hands now."

Bekah looked at Lt. Carson. "We don't know. There's a good chance he's not going to make it," she said.

"This is a nightmare," Bekah pleaded. "The same nightmare I had when David died. Oh, please." She sobbed. "Please, don't take him from me."

She gestured for the women to bring her closer. She looked down at the bandages—nothing but bandages and a small slit for his mouth—and whispered, "My love."

It was then that she saw his finger move against the mattress. It was the only part of him that was not bandaged. It moved rhythmically. Deliberately. She stared at it in uncomprehending confusion until at last she realized what he was doing.

It's Morse code.

I L-O-V-E Y-O-U.

"Father," Bekah said to the priest. "Marry us. Right now. He's talking. In Morse code. And I know it. I'll do his vows."

The priest hesitated. She said, "Father, he may be dying. And . . . and I don't want to regret the things I didn't do."

Y-E-S.

"This is very unusual."

"Wars are very unusual, Father," Aunt Miriam said. She opened her handbag, muttering, "You can't imagine how many hypodermic needles this thing can hold," then cried out with triumph and showed Bekah the box containing Ma'am's ring.

"I never told you the story that went with this ring," she said to Bekah. "This ring was carved for Ma'am by a poor, young seafaring man. It was to be her wedding ring. She accepted him. But then she got a second proposal. It was the wealthy Mr. Jones, and she married him for his money. It was a decision she regretted all her life."

Bekah took the ring and clutched it against her chest.

Scott began to cough. His chest moved up and down. Lt. Carson stepped forward and swabbed out his mouth. She looked anxiously at Bekah.

"Father, quickly," she said. "Marry us, please."

"All right," the priest decided. He picked up a leather-bound book. "In the name of the Father, and the Son, and the Holy Ghost. Amen."

Bekah's fingers tapped gently against Scott's.

A-N-D T-H-E H-O-L-Y G-H-O-S-T A-M-E-N.

In her mind's eye, she saw David riding Lono across the sky, galloping across clouds, laughing and handsome and free. He saw a rainbow and pointed to it and said, "Catch it, Beks!" Then he disappeared.

Forever, Bekah knew. She had finally let him go.

Scott coughed harder. His chest began to spasm as he hacked uncontrollably.

"Read faster," Bekah said. Tears streamed down her face, but she was at peace within herself. Whatever happened, she would have this moment. Scott would have it, too. Whatever came next, they had faced it together.

She was not afraid to love him any longer.

His coughing made the bed shake. Bekah held on to his finger while Lt. Carson tried to swab something out of his mouth.

"Miracles happen, my dear," the priest said, making the sign of the cross over Scott and then over her. "Don't doubt it."

She smiled through the tears and the blood. "I don't doubt it for a moment, Father," she said firmly, "and neither does my husband."

Scott's fingers tapped against hers. "I L-O-V-E—"

Bekah waited for the rest.

If she had to stand here until eternity, Mrs. DeAngelo would wait for the rest.

192

Author's Note

I was very pleased to have the opportunity to write about a very important event in Hawaiian and American history. During this time period, my grandfather was the head of Kula Sanatorium on Maui. His name was Kenneth P. Jones, and he wrote a history of the Sanatorium for its thirty-year anniversary. My grandmother, Lucile M. Jones, raised two children on the island, my father and my aunt. I have several photos of them dressed in the Spanish-style costumes I mention in my book.

My aunt, Karen Beth (Betsy) Ingle, was a student at Punahou on the island of Oahu and saw the attack occur. She was not reunited with my grandparents until almost a week later, when a ship traveling from Oahu to Maui took her home. My father, Kenneth P. Jones III, was a medical student at the University of Michigan. I still have the telegram my grandparents sent to him, assuring him that the family was safe.

Today, one of my sisters lives on Oahu. I myself

attended the University of Hawaii at Manoa. We have been to all the places mentioned in the book, including the beautiful Pearl Harbor Naval Base. It tugged at my heart to stand above the sunken battleship *Arizona*, preserved as a memorial and final resting place for the over 1,000 men who died aboard her.

The gallant *Nevada* was repaired, modernized, and returned to service. She participated in battles at Iowa Jima, Okinawa, and throughout the Pacific theater. Her officers and crew received more Medals of Honor and Navy Crosses than the crew of any other naval vessel before or since.

After the end of World War II, the *Nevada* was selected to serve as the target ship for an atomic bomb test at Bikini Atoll. Incredibly, she survived both the atomic explosion and underwater explosions connected with the test. Two years later, the Navy tried to sink the *Nevada*. She was towed 65 miles southwest of Hawaii and loaded with explosives. She still did not sink. Guided missiles were aimed at her, and missed the target. The battleship *Iowa* and three cruises bombarded her with shells, but still she remained afloat. Navy fighters were brought in, but even they couldn't sink the *Nevada*. Finally, Navy torpedo bombers succeeded where others had failed: an aerial torpedo struck the *Nevada* and she eventually, finally sank.

Today, a nuclear submarine carries her proud

name. My grandparents, father, and aunt have all passed on as well. When Aunt Betsy died, my cousins and I threw a *lei* into the ocean, wishing her *aloha* and Godspeed.

I wish the same for all the courageous souls who lived and fought aboard BB-36 U.S.S. *Nevada*, and for the survivors of the Pearl Harbor attack who shared their remarkable stories.

About the Author

NANCY HOLDER is the author of 45 novels for young adults, children, and adults, and over 200 short stories. A charter member of the Romance Writers of America, seven of her romances appeared on the Waldenbooks Romance Bestseller List. She has won four Bram Stoker awards, the highest accolade in the horror field, and her work has been translated into over two dozen languages. She has written many novels for the *Buffy the Vampire Slayer* and *Angel* TV series, as well as a science fiction trilogy called *Gambler's Star* for Avon.

. . . A GIRL BORN
WITHOUT THE FEAR GENE

FEARLESS™

A SERIES BY
FRANCINE PASCAL

FROM POCKET PULSE
PUBLISHED BY POCKET BOOKS

3029

I'm 16,
I'm a witch,
and I still have
to go to school?

Look for a new title
every month
Based on the hit TV series

From Archway Paperbacks
Published by Pocket Books